Jotunheimen

A Solo Female Wanderer Hiking Guide

Jotunheimen, A Solo Female Wanderer Hiking Guide. Copyright 2025 by Sarah Rowe. For more information about this hiking guide and others, email hi@solofemalewanderer.com

A portion of the proceeds from the sale of this guide are donated to DNT to support their work maintaining the trail system and cabins.

Maps are from Kartverket under its Creative Commons license.

Introduction

Jotunheimen translates to the home of the giants. And it's accurate - it's the park in Norway with most of Norway's peaks over 2,000 meters. It has alpine peaks, deep lakes, wildflowers, snowfields, and everything in between.

But one of the joys of Jotunheimen is that there's actually hiking for every level. You can choose easier hikes that go along the side of a lake or an excursion to the top of Norway's highest peak. And the hikes go in between serviced cabins that provide comfortable beds and three course dinners.

It's Norway's most popular national park, with good reason. Ready to explore?

Table of Contents

Routes

Length (km)	Elevation Gain (m)	Elevation Drop (m)	Hours (from ut.no)
21.8	969	582	8
13.3	1,076	1,086	6 to 8
16.3	906	904	8
19.0	1,069	694	5 to 7
10.5	739	725	6
17.2	1,378	1,672	9
15.9	365	663	5
13.8	1,754	1,754	8
15.9	458	147	5
23.9	752	864	9
8.8	603	603	4
10.6	363	327	3.5
18.8	338	742	8
18.9	754	185	6
14.4	839	126	5 to 7
14.0	226	803	5
11.9	363	1,217	6
10.2	551	700	5
17.2	330	930	6
18.2	232	839	6
24.8	1,129	1,015	6
30.3	753	919	6
15.6	77	517	5
13.8	335	716	6
22.3	1,061	654	8
15.9	747	745	6
22.5	684	430	6
11.3	675	233	5
19.5	671	671	6
20.3	749	748	8
14.0	113	113	3.5
14.1	493	553	5
15.9	466	526	5.5
2.7	77	464	4
12.5	680	680	6

Suggested Route Combinations

The best way to enjoy Jotunheimen is to go from cabin to cabin. While it's possible to stay in a single cabin and do day hikes, the Norwegian hiking network is best set up for multiday, cabin to cabin hikes. Some sample multiday routes below:

6 Days in Jotunheimen's Peaks

This is a classic tour through Jotunheimen - and the most visited route on my blog. It winds through Jotunheimen, hitting all of the classic sights. Add on Galdhøpiggen and Kyrkja to really get the summit experience.

From	Page	Distance (km)	Up (meters)	Down (meters)	Time
Gjendesheim to Glitterheim	10	21.8	969	582	8 hours
Glitterheim to Spiterstulen - Glittertinden	20	17.2	1,378	1,672	8 hours
Spiterstulen to Leirvassbu	26	15.9	458	147	5 hours
Leirvassbu to Gjendebu	34	18.8	338	742	8 hours
Gjendebu to Memurubu (Bukkelægret)	18	10.5	739	725	6 hours
Memurubu to Gjendesheim (Besseggen)	12	13.3	1,076	1,086	6 to 8 hours

Omveien - Jotunheimen portion

Omveien means "the detour" and is one of the Norwegian Trekking Association (DNT's) recently developed long tours. Omveien starts in Lillehammer and goes to the Sognefjord, but it's possible to do just the Jotunheimen portion. This route loops through most of Jotunheimen

From	Page	Distance (km)	Up (meters)	Down (meters)	Time
Gjendesheim to Glitterheim	10	21.8	969	582	8 hours
Glitterheim to Spiterstulen - Glittertinden	20	17.2	1,378	1,672	8 hours
Spiterstulen to Leirvassbu	26	15.9	458	147	5 hours
Leirvassbu to Olavsbu	32	10.6	363	327	3.5 hours
Olavsbu - Rauddalen to Skogadalsbøen	48	18.2	232	839	6 hours
Skogadalsbøen to Vettismorki	44	10.2	551	700	5 hours
Vettismorki to Hjelle and Øvre Årdal	76	2.7	77	464	4 hours

Round trip in the Gjende Alps

Looking to get in the less traveled side of Jotunheimen? The Gjende Alps are much quieter than the mountains to the north, and you can stay in small, self-service cabins rather than larger serviced cabins.

From	Page	Distance (km)	Up (meters)	Down (meters)	Time
Bygdin to Torfinnsbu	70	14.0	113	113	3.5 hours
Torfinnsbu to Gjendebu	72	14.1	493	553	5 hours
Gjendebu to Fondsbu	74	15.9	526	466	5.5 hours
Fondsbu to Torfinnsbu	68	20.3	749	748	8 hours

Gjendesheim to Glitterheim

21.8 km	969 meters	582 meters	8 hours
13.5 miles	3,178 feet	1,909 feet	Challenging

The route for today starts by going up towards Gjendehalsen, passing by the paths that branch off to Besseggen and Memurubu. There's a climb at the beginning of the day as you pass by the trail that branches off towards Besseggen. It can be a bit rocky in this section.

Keep going towards the north, passing by the ends of a few lakes. You should have a great view out towards Glittertinden through this section.

Pass over the bridge at the end of the Russvatnet, then turn towards the west, gently climbing along the riverside and then up onto a bowl. There is one bridge here that is a hanging bridge that really bounces as you cross it - it's stable, but it's a bit nerve wracking to go over.

The terrain becomes more open and rocky here as the trail climbs away from the river. The trail continues to gain elevation up to a saddle in between eastern and western Hestlægerhøe ("Austre og Vestre Hestlægerhøe").

After that, drop down towards Glitterheim, first in rocky terrain and then in partially wet terrain. The cabin is further away than it appears from the mountain, and there's a little bit of a detour towards the end.

My hiking notes

This is a long hike with some sneaky elevation in it - there's not a climb like there is on some of the other days here, but I definitely felt it by the end of the day. I found the end the mentally toughest - you can see Glitterheim with a few kilometers left to go.

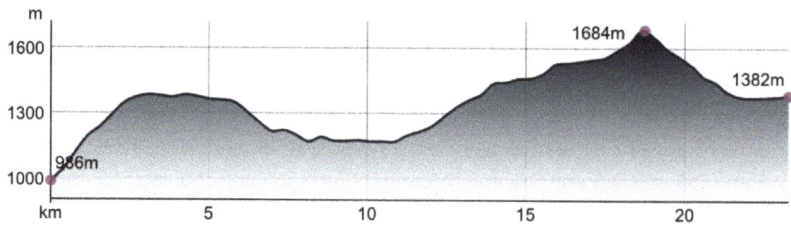

There were lots of lakes and rivers underway to fill up a water bottle in, plus views onto a lot more lakes

11

Besseggen

13.3 km 8.3 miles	1,076 meters 3,529 feet	1,086 meters 3,526 feet	6-8 hours Very challenging

This is Norway's most done hike and one of National Geographic's ten hikes to do in your life. There are people who come to Norway just to do this hike - so you should definitely add it to your list.

I recommend starting the hike from Memurubu so that you don't have to worry about catching a boat back to Gjendesheim at the end of the day. Either spend the night at Memurubu or take the first boat from Gjendesheim in the morning to start the hike. From Memurubu, the hike starts with a very steep climb on a dirt trail for about two kilometers. Here, you pass by a trail going towards Glitterheim. Continue towards the east, in what quickly becomes more rocky and rolling terrain.

You'll pass signs in this section that let you know how you're pacing, and whether you should turn around based on your speed.

Continue climbing. The trail passes by a small lake, with spectacular views over the Gjendevatnet to your right. Continue following the trail over a small descent until you reach the side of the Bessvatnet lake.

From here, the trail continues on a short but very steep section. This section requires climbing on hands and knees, and there are drop offs on each side. Put away hiking poles if you have them and make sure to keep your center of gravity low as you climb. It's a short section, a few hundred meters, that's particularly challenging.

If it is raining or you are not comfortable, you can instead choose to do a longer loop around Bessvatnet to meet the trail from Glitterheim. That trail is not easy - it still goes on rocky terrain - but does not have a steep drop off on either side.

From the top of the scramble, stop and look back to see the classic view with Gjendevatnet on one side and Bessvatnet on the other.

After this, continue along a flat section for about a kilometer. This section is a wide trail on top of the mountain and easy to walk. After that, start the drop down towards Gjendesheim. This is quite steep and goes over rocky terrain. Make sure to stay on the trail - there are several areas where people have tried to create shortcuts in the terrain. End at Gjendesheim.

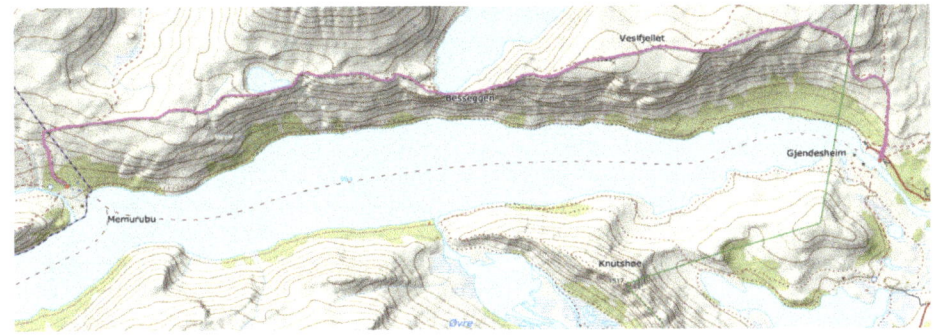

My notes

I thought that this hike was going to be overhyped just given its sheer popularity. It was not. The views were absolutely spectacular, and it's well worth doing. That being said, I would only do it in good weather - the scramble is difficult if the rocks are wet, and it can be crowded with people who are not experienced in the mountains.

Make sure to have clothes that are suitable for both high elevation and lower down. You'll sweat a lot on the way up and want something warmer to change into for the flatter sections along the top of the ridge.

If you're a fast hiker and have good weather, think about starting in the afternoon rather than the morning - I had many fewer people on the route because I started around one rather than in the morning with the boat.

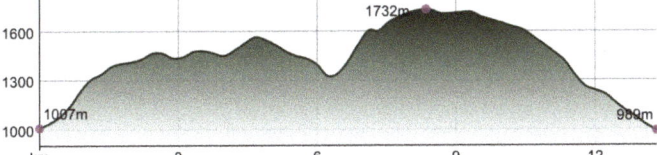

Sikkilsdalsseter to Gjendesheim

16.3 km
10.1 miles

906 meters
2,971 feet

904 meters
2,965 feet

8 hours
Challenging

Over Sikkilsdalsvatnet:

Start the day by going along the Sikkilsdals lake. Parts of the trail have large rocks that may require a bit of scrambling over. At the end of the lake, the trail will begin to climb up towards the Sikkilsdalsskardet, with a view towards Jotunheimen.

After the small climb, start to follow a path through a combination of open area and forest towards Maurvangen. The path is easy to follow, but there can be a few streams to rock hop across if there's been rain recently.

Eventually, the route drops down to Maurvangen. Walk through the camping area towards the reception area, then cross over the pedestrian bridge to the road. Cross the road and turn right, then turn left onto the road towards Gjendesheim.

From here, it's about half an hour on a road to Gjendesheim. There is a trail beside the road to Gjendesheim - look on the right for a turnoff to catch it

Over Sikkilsdalshø (map and elevation profile)

I chose to go over Sikkilsdalshø, which takes about 8 hours and has quite a bit more climb. To do that trail, start by climbing up from behind Sikkilsdalsseter. The trail goes through a combination of forest and open mountain areas, then reaches a lake and goes along the lake for a bit.

After the lake, there's a final rocky climb - the path isn't super wide, so watch your footing. At the top, there's a spectacular view out towards Jotunheimen. After that, the trail drops elevation through first rocky and then dirt terrain. It's a bit steep but not terrible, and the views are fantastic. Eventually, the path starts to go through the forest and then meets up with the trail coming via Sikkilsdalsvatnet.

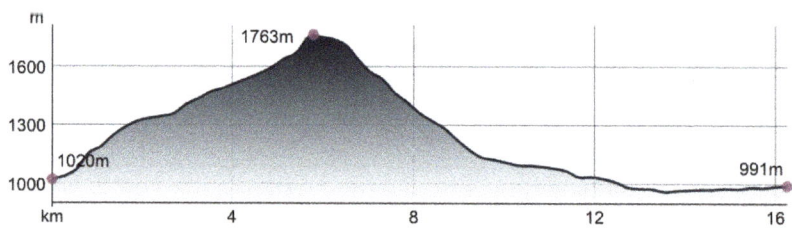

My notes:

I absolutely loved the route over Sikkildalshø - the views were spectacular. I highly recommend it if you've got good weather. There are a few false summits on the way and a little bit of scrambling, but it's not bad.

It's longer than I mentally expected from where the two trails meet up to Gjendesheim. Try to find the trail alongside the road on the way to Gjendesheim if you can - it's much more pleasant than the road. Alternatively, you might be able to catch the shuttle bus from the boat parking area to the cabin.

Memurubu to Glitterheim

19.0 km
11.8 miles

1,069 meters
3,506 feet

694 meters
2,276 feet

8 hours
Challenging

The route starts from Memurubu with a very steep climb along the trail towards Besseggen. The trail is initially dirt and very easy to follow, but it's an intense climb. After about 1.5 kilometers of straight climb, the trail forks. Follow the trail that heads north towards Glitterheim. From here, the terrain starts to become very rocky.

The trail flattens out and goes along the north side of the Russvatnet lake. After 8.5 kilometers of total hiking, the trail starts to climb up again, first gradually and then more steeply, leaving the side of the lake and heading north. The trail climbs up towards a bridge over Blåtjønnåe - the bridge has been replaced in the past five years, so follow cairns to the bridge, which is at about 1240 meters above sea level. Older maps might not be accurate.

After crossing the bridge, continue climbing, following the trail towards the north in rocky terrain. The trail climbs until it reaches about 1685 meters of elevation and crosses over Vestre Hestægerhøe. After crossing over the ridge, start to drop in rocky terrain down to Glitterheim.

After that, drop down towards Glitterheim, first in rocky terrain and then in partially wet terrain. The cabin is further away than it appears from the mountain, and the trail loops around some small lakes as it gets close to the cabin.

My notes

The terrain here can be surprisingly rocky in parts - I found balancing on the rocky terrain to be more of a challenge than the climb itself. Take it slowly, and don't plan to make great time.

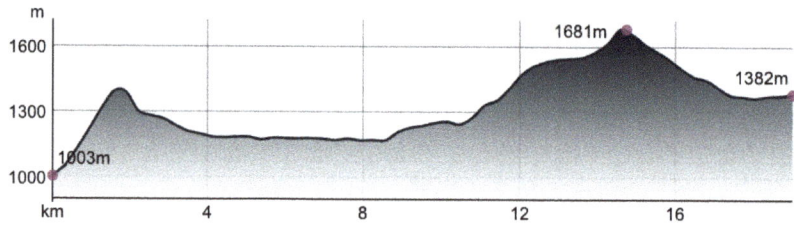

Take your time on the rocks on this hike, especially if it's rained recently. Flat doesn't mean easy

Gjendebu to Memurubu

| 10.5 km | 739 meters | 725 meters | 6 hours |
| 6.5 miles | 2,424 feet | 2,378 feet | Challenging |

Today's route starts along the Gjende lake. Walk from the cabin to the boat stop, then follow the trail along the side of the river. This is flat and easy to walk. After 4km, you will start the climb up to Bukkelægeret.

It's a steep climb, with some sections where there are drop offs. There are parts where there are wires to help navigate the trail, and this can be very difficult if it's rained recently. It's about 1.5 kilometers of very intense climb before the trail starts to flatten out along the top of a ridge. Turn back and get a great view of the lake before heading onto the path. For the next three kilometers, the trail is flat or gently declining as it passes through a section with flowers if you're lucky and small lakes.

The path isn't too rocky until you get close to the drop down to Memurubu. The decline here is quite steep, but there is only a small section that has a drop off on one side. Eventually, the trail crosses over a river and ends at Memurubu.

My notes

I loved this hike, although I wouldn't recommend it if you're not comfortable with using chains at the beginning. I would also strongly recommend this direction rather than the other - it was easier to go up the steep section than down.

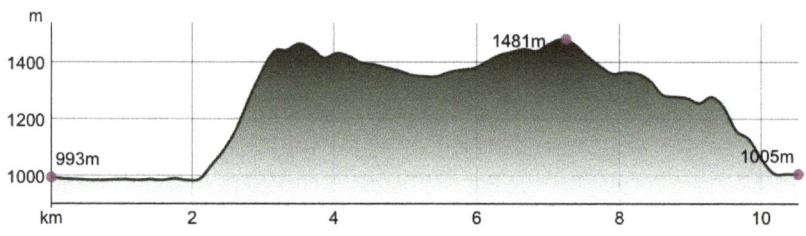

The views start and end looking over Gjende lake, with spectacular views back into north Jotunheimen in the middle. If you're lucky, you're get wildflowers too (I didn't, unfortunately)

Glitterheim to Spiterstulen - Glittertinden

17.2 km
10.7 miles

1,378 meters
4,520 feet

1,672 meters
5,484 feet

9 hours
Very Challenging

Ready to take on Norway's second highest peak?

Start the day by taking the trail directly behind Glitterheim. It starts out on dirt trails, which quickly change into rockier trails. Continue climbing, taking your time to balance on the rocks as you go. As the trail gets closer to the top, it starts to cross across snow fields. Follow the marked trail and stay away from the side of the snowfield.

There is no marker for the summit, but I recommend sitting down anywhere on the snow and enjoying the view. There's a stunning view back towards the surrounding peaks.

The trail down to Spiterstulen is easy to find, but it's quite steep and rocky for the first few kilometers. I found it took as long as the hike towards the top. After dropping through the rocky section, the trail continues through a flat section for a couple of kilometers before turning slightly and starting the hike down along the wall towards Spiterstulen.

The trail hits the road - turn left and follow it to Spiterstulen.

My notes

I loved this hike. The view is spectacular, and while it's quite a climb, it's not too technically challenging. I took a nice nap towards the top and had a very slow lunch there.

This is a popular day tour from Glitterheim, so you may see quite a few other people out with much smaller backpacks. Make sure that you have enough layers, because it is cold and usually snowing at the top. And if you're not going all the way to Spiterstulen, borrow a sled from Glitterheim for the fastest possible way down the mountain.

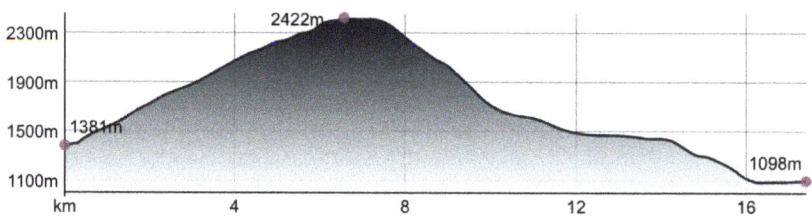

Glitterheim to Spiterstulen - not Glittertinden

15.9 km
9.8 miles

365 meters
1,197 feet

663 meters
2,175 feet

5 hours
Challenging

This is a slightly easier alternative to going over Glittertinden from Glitterheim to Spiterstulen. It's easier in that there's much less elevation gain, but it's in no way an easy trail - the terrain is rocky, and there are places where you'll need to rock hop across rivers.

Start by crossing over a summer bridge over the Steinbuelve, going into the Veodalen valley. The first 4.5 kilometers are a gentle climb through the valley. The trail crosses over a few rivers that may need to be rock hopped or waded across, particularly if there's been recent snow melt.

From here, the trail starts to curve more towards the north and steeply climb up towards right under the Veslglupen. The trail goes past a series of small lakes, heading west, then curves towards the northwest again.

At about 8.7 total kilometers, there's another river that requires wading. Cross that river, then continue to follow the trail, gently dropping elevation. Eventually, the trail meets up with the trail coming over Glittertinden. From here, follow the trail along the side of a valley and then down to Spiterstulen.

My notes

I recommend doing the trail over Glittertinden if you can - the views are absolutely spectacular. This isn't to shame this trail, which is also beautiful, but Glittertinden was one of my favorite hikes in Norway.

If there's been a lot of recent snow melt or rain, ask at the cabin about how much wading is required. It varies a lot depending on the time of year and recent weather.

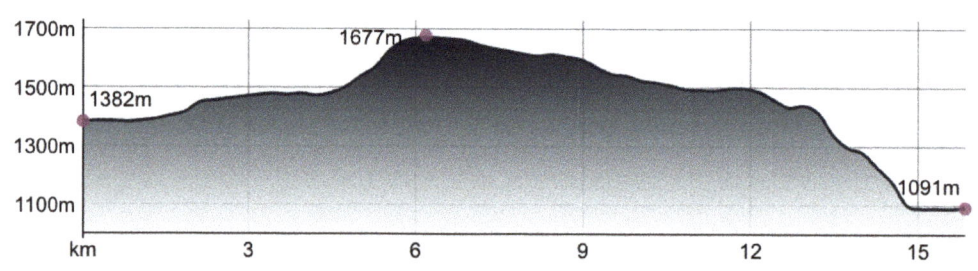

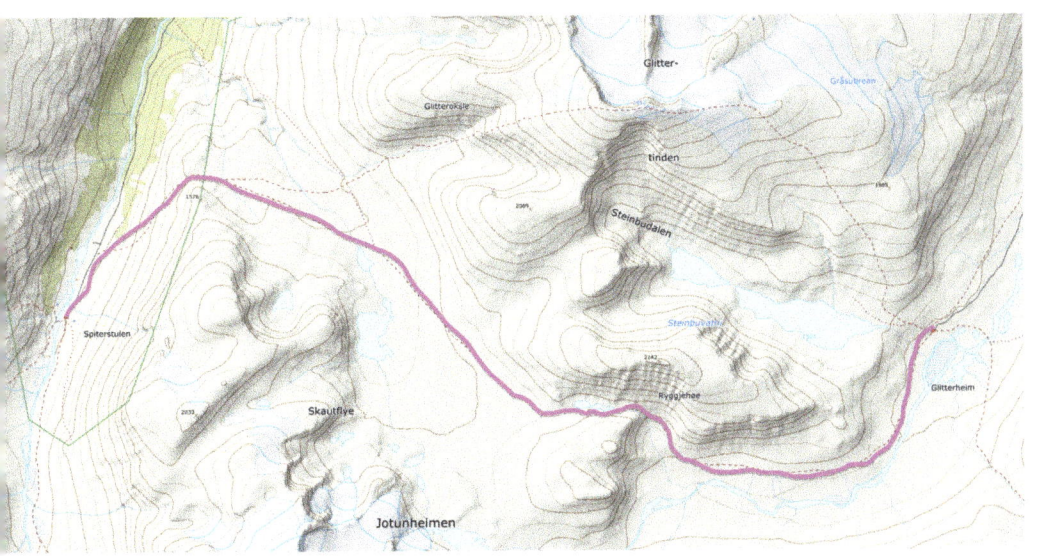

The last drop down to Spiterstulen can be mentally tough if you're not expecting it - be prepared for it to feel longer than it looks on the map

Spiterstulen to Galdhøpiggen

13.8 km
8.6 miles

1,754 meters
5,753 feet

1,754 meters
5,753 feet

8 hours
Challenging

Galdhøpiggen is Norway's highest mountain and an important part of Norwegian culture - its elevation, 2469, is immediately recognizable to many people. (UT.no claims it's recognizable for all Norwegians, but that might be a stretch.)

It's a straightforward, though challenging, hike up from Spiterstulen to the summit. Take the trail from Spiterstulen, cross the river, and immediately start climbing. The beginning of the day is on dirt trails, which quickly turn into rocky terrain. Continue to climb and you will likely encounter snowfields. Fortunately, this is a well-traveled path, so there should be clear footprints marking the trail.

Continue to steadily climb until you reach the summit. There's a small cafe at the summit that offers sausages, coffee, and other warm drinks. Stop here and enjoy the view. When you're done, turn around and go down the way you came.

My notes

This is a very easy trail to follow, but it is quite a lot of climbing. It is no way an easy hike, but you'll see plenty of families with children on the way.

There are two false summits on the way - I kept thinking that I could see the peak and was almost there, only to realize that there was another peak hiding behind the first. Mentally prepare yourself for that.

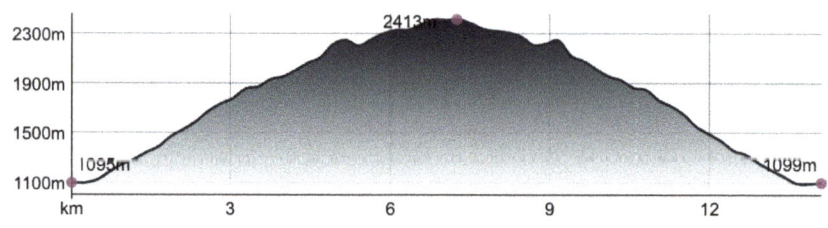

If you have snowfields, you can save some time on the descent by sliding down on your butt. It is not elegant, but it is a lot of fun.

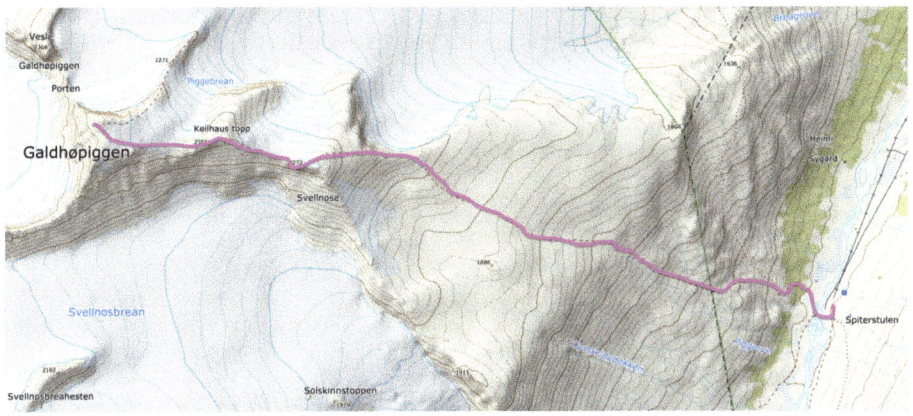

25

Spiterstulen to Leirvassbu

15.9 km	458 meters	147 meters	5 hours
9.9 miles	1,502 feet	482 feet	Challenging

The route starts going south from Spiterstulen, following the river. The trail starts as a dirt trail that's pretty easy to follow, but there are a few sections where it's rocky. Keep going south, gradually adding elevation.

At about six kilometers in, there's a fork in the trail. Turn towards the west and follow the trail going to Leirvassbu - there's a sign. From here, the trail can get rocky. As you get close to Leirvassbu, you'll circle around a lake, Leirvatnet, towards the cabin. This area can have quite a few bugs if it's still.

If it's rained recently, there may be some areas where you have to wade or jump across rocks. I found those mostly in the second half of the hike - there were planks put out for the sections in the first part of the hike.

My notes

This is a good day to make into a bit of a rest day in the middle of the hike, especially if you've added in Galdhøpiggen the day before. You're up at considerably higher elevation for a lot of the day - when I hiked it, the lakes were still mostly frozen, and the snowmelt made the rivers very high.

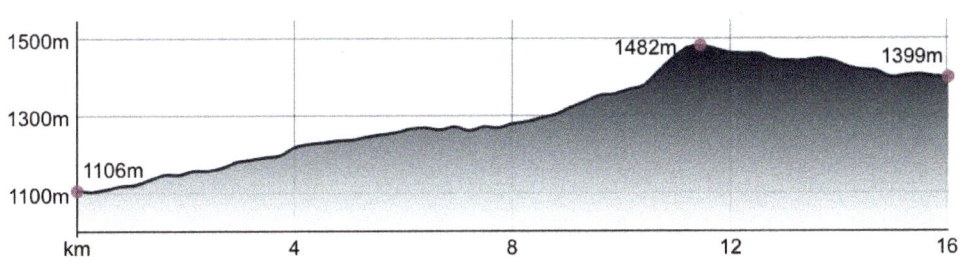

Spiterstulen to Gjendebu

23.9 km
14.8 miles

752 meters
2,467 feet

864 meters
2,834 feet

9 hours
Challenging

The route starts by going south from Spiterstulen, following the river. The trail starts as a dirt trail that's pretty easy to follow, but there are a few sections where it's rocky. Keep going south, gradually adding elevation.

At about six kilometers in, there's a fork in the trail. Turn towards the southeast and start to follow the trail towards Gjendebu through the Urdadalen. The trail starts to climb steeply for the next two kilometers in very rocky terrain - take your time. Keep climbing until you reach the high point of the trail at 1,663 meters. Take a rest here before starting a gradual and then steeper descent, finally meeting up with the trail running from Leirvassbu to Gjendebu.

From here, the trail continues to drop, with flattish sections interspersed with steep drops, until it enters the green valley near Gjendebu.

My notes

The terrain on this one is tough - it's very rocky. I highly recommend shoes that will keep your ankles from getting scraped up. I didn't find poles to be particularly useful, since I was rock hopping for a lot of the hike.

Galdhøpiggen
Nørdre
Illåbrean
Svellnos-
brean
Spiterstulen
Skautflye
Steinbuvatnet
Ryggjehøe
Glitterheim
Tverråtinden
Bukkehøe
Tverråbrean
Jotunheimen
Leirhøe
Styggehøe
Søre Illåbrean
Visa
Veobrean
Styggehøe
Store
Veotinden
Store
Blåtjønn-
holet
Bukkeholstinden
Hellstugu-
høe
Store
Søre
Urdadalen
Grønbakkan
Midtre
Memurutinden
Tverrbottindan
Hellstugu-
tindan
Austre
Memurubrean
Surtningssu-
oksle
Leirvassbu
Urdadals-
tindan
Kyrkja
Visbrean
Vestre
Memurubrean
Surtningssue
Visbreatinden
Memurudalen
Semel-
tinden
Semeltjønne
Høgvagl-
tindane
Hinnåtjønne
Skarddalseggje
Memurubu
Memuru-
tunga
Storådalshøe
Skarddalsvatnet
Gjende
Olavsbu
Store
Rauddalseggje
Storådalen
Rauddalen
Gjendebu
Gjende
Høgdebrotet
Tjønnholstinden
tinden

m
1600
1300
1000
km
5
10
15
20
1668m
1091m
988m

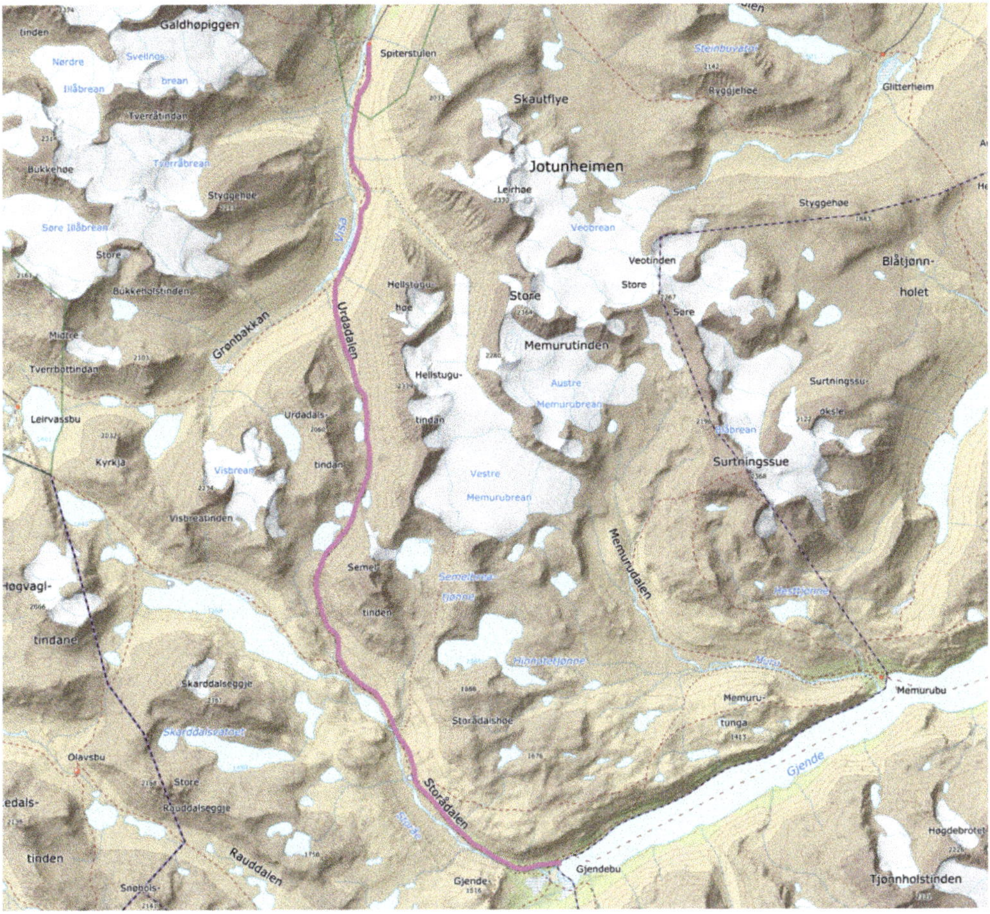

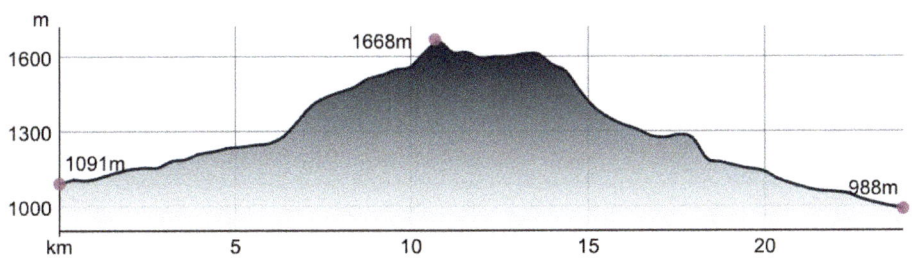

Leirvassbu to Kyrkja

8.8 km
5.5 miles

603 meters
1,978 feet

603 meters
1,978 feet

4 hours
Very challenging

Kyrkja is an iconic mountain top in Norway - it spikes up from the surrounding terrain. It's a spectacular trip, but it's only recommended for adults and those with mountain experience - it's very steep, and there's quite a bit of scrambling at the end.

The first two kilometers of the trail follows the road from Leirvassbu towards Olavsbu. The trail can be a bit hard to find here, and there are often still snowfields. After about two kilometers, there is a turnoff to the left for the trail up to Kyrkja. It's not marked with the red T, but there are clear cairns to show the trail.

The terrain in this section is extremely rocky and steep. As you get close to the top, you will need to scramble on all fours through some sections. The trail is narrow, with steep drop offs on both sides. I don't recommend this hike in the rain.

Once you reach the top, take a look around and then go back the way you came.

My notes

I left my backpack and poles next to a cairn when I still had about 400 meters of elevation to climb. That was a great idea - the last section is extremely steep, and I felt like I was clinging to the rocks on the side of the mountain. Not having the backpack made me more flexible and kept my center of gravity closer to the mountain.

The view from the top was well worth it, but this is definitely not a hike to do if you aren't comfortable with scrambling or are scared of heights.

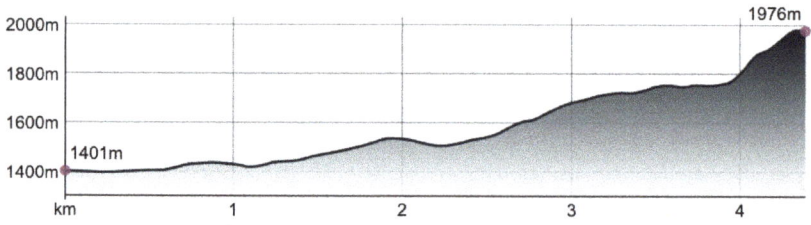

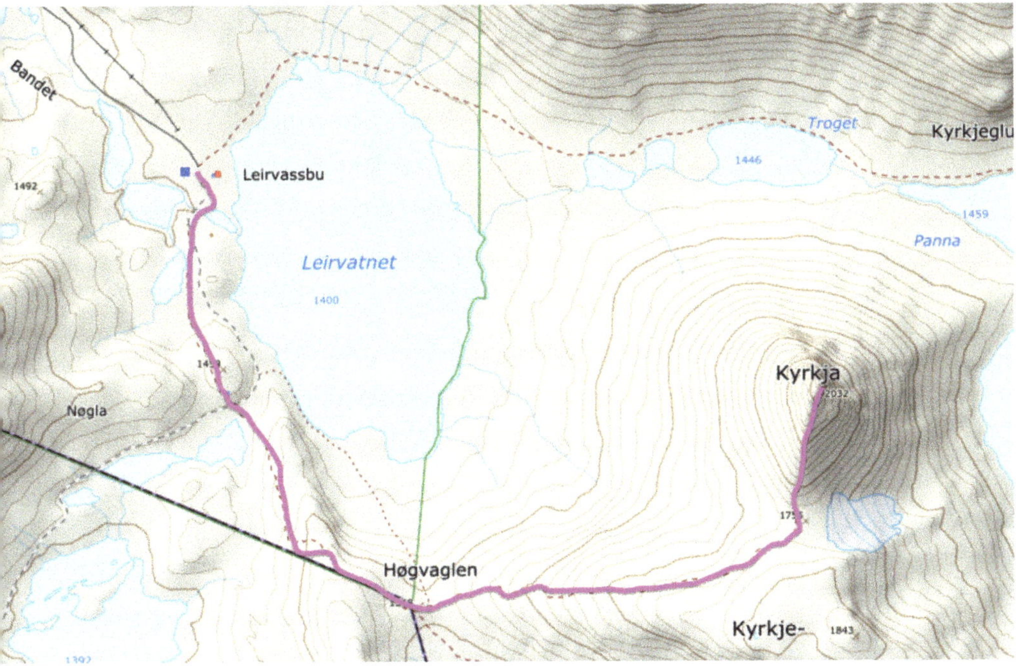

Bandet

Troget

Kyrkjeglu

Leirvassbu

1446

1492

1459

Panna

Leirvatnet

1400

Kyrkja

2032

Nøgla

1759

Høgvaglen

Kyrkje-

1843

1392

I was treated to a fighter jet flyover when I finally reached the top of the scramble - quite a surprise after hiking in silence

Leirvassbu to Olavsbu

10.6 km
6.6 miles

363 meters
1,191 feet

327 meters
1,073 feet

3.5 hours
Challenging

My hiking notes

The day starts by going along a construction road from Leirvassbu towards Sognefjellshytta and Skogadalsbøen. The path is a bit tricky to find in this section, especially if there are still snowfields on the ground. I ended up getting a little off path and catching the path again about a kilometer in. Keep checking UT.

At about two kilometers in, the trail passes by the turnoff to Kyrkja. From here, it passes by two lakes, upper and lower Høgvagltjønnen, before reaching a fork. Take the trail on the right towards Olavsbu, not the one on the left towards Gjendebu. From here, it's six kilometers in rocky terrain. There's a bit of a climb, then a gradual downhill until you reach Olavsbu. Olavsbu feels like it comes out of nowhere, so don't get discouraged if you don't see the cabin until a few hundred meters away.

There were still a lot of snowfields left when I did this hike, and there were a few sections where I had to rock hop across running water. My poles were definitely helpful.

My notes

You can combine this hike with the hike to Skogadalsbøen if you get an early start or are feeling really good - the next day is all downhill.

Olavsbu is an enormous self-service cabin - it's DNT Oslo's biggest self-service cabin. There's usually a hyttevakt, or a volunteer who helps make sure the cabin runs smoothly, there if you have questions.

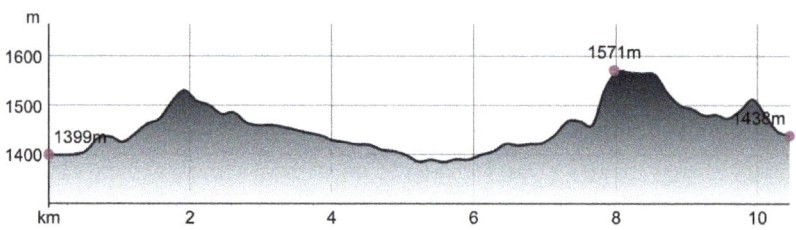

If it's rained a lot recently, there might be sections that require wading on this hike. It's either easy or a real pain depending on how much water there is in the rivers

Leirvassbu to Gjendebu

18.8 km
11.6 miles

338 meters
1,109 feet

742 meters
2,434 feet

8 hours
Challenging

The day starts by going along a construction road from Leirvassbu towards Sognefjellshytta and Skogadalsbøen. The path is a bit tricky to find in this section, especially if there are still snowfields on the ground. I ended up getting a little off path and catching the path again about a kilometer in. Keep checking UT.

At about two kilometers in, the trail passes by the turnoff to Kyrkja. From here, it passes by two lakes, upper and lower Høgvagltjønnen, before reaching a fork. Take the path on the left towards Gjendebu (not towards Olavsbu).

The path goes along the side of the Langavatnet ("the long lake") in sometimes quite rocky terrain. Continue heading south along the trail towards another lake, then pass by Hellefossen, a small waterfall. From here, the trail becomes progressively less rocky as you drop into the Storådalen valley and then to Gjendebu along the side of the lake.

My notes

The first part of this hike is definitely the most rocky and difficult - once you're past that, it becomes progressively easier. There are no steep sections in the hike, so it's a nice rest for your legs if you're doing a summit tour in the area.

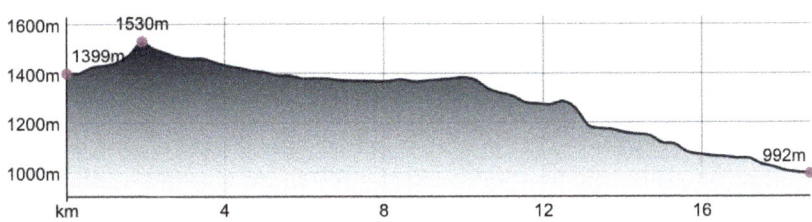

Gjendebu doesn't have phone service, so check the
weather and screenshot it on the way. You may also
want to book a bed at Gjendebu underway if you're
in the peak summer season - Gjendebu is a launching
point for Besseggen and Bukkelægret and can get
crowded.

Skogadalsbøen to Leirvassbu

18.9 km
11.7 miles

754 meters
2,473 feet

185 meters
607 feet

6 hours
Challenging

The route today starts by going north through the valley from Skogadalsbøen, past the meeting point with the trail coming down from Fannårkhytta. The first two kilometers are a gentle climb.

From here, the trail turns towards the east and then starts to climb through the Storutladalen. This is steeper than the section before as you climb through the forest. The trail will start to come rocky through this section and continue to climb. At about seven kilometers in, take the bridge over the river and continue along the north side of the river. Eventually, the trail passes by Gravdalsdammen and continues to climb in rocky terrain. It's a steady climb through this section

At about eighteen kilometers in / one kilometer to go, the trail reaches an intersection with the trail coming from Olavsbu. Continue to follow the trail north for an additional kilometer to reach Leirvassbu. This section can be a little bit hard to navigate, particularly if there are still snowfields.

My notes

I loved this hike - the views in the valley at the beginning of the day were much better than I expected from being so low in the valley. It's a steady climb throughout the day, so make sure to pace yourself.

If it's a hot day and you need to cool off, the bridge where the trail splits from the trail to Olavsbu has a great swimming hole.

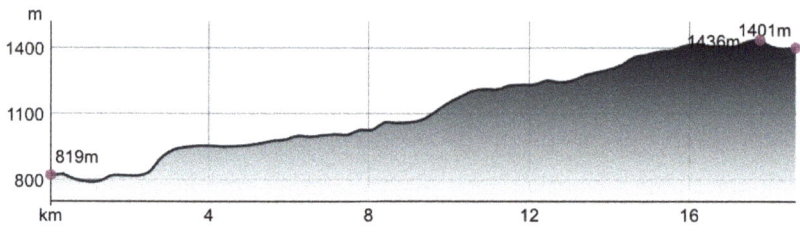

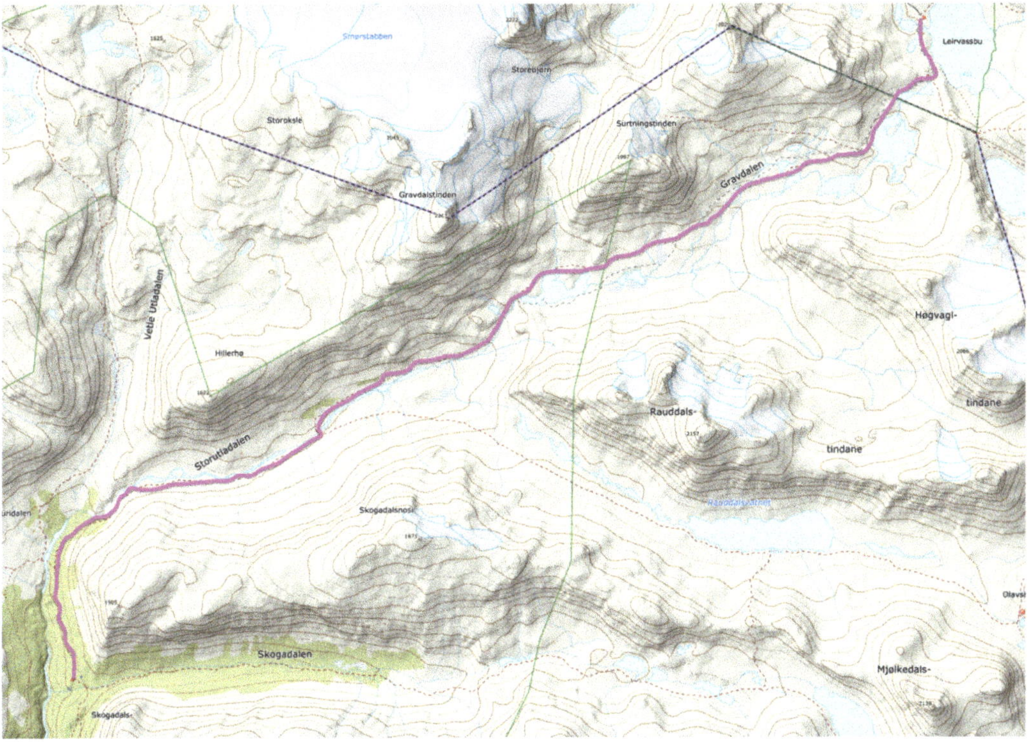

If you're lucky, you'll see the iconic view of Kyrkja over the lake as you round into Leirvassbu at the end of the day

Sognefjellshytta to Fannaråkhytta

14.4 km
9.0 miles

839 meters
2,752 feet

126 meters
413 feet

5 to 7 hours
Challenging

Today starts with a relatively short hike to the base of the Fannårk glacier, over a pretty straightforward trail. There's not a ton of elevation gain on the first part, and the trail is much less rocky than the previous days.

You'll meet the guide and the rest of the group going up the glacier at the base of the glacier after about six kilometers of hiking. The trail can be hard to spot for the last kilometer, so follow other people if you can. Once you're at the base of the glacier, wait for the guides to come down and give everyone instructions, then you'll then go over the glacier roped in together. If you're lucky enough to have good weather, the views are spectacular.

Once you finish crossing the glacier, there are two kilometers left of climb to reach the cabin. This section is rockier than the morning,.You need to book Fannaråken in advance, since they have a very limited number of beds. You'll also need to book guiding over the glacier, which you can do either at the reception at Sognefjellshytta or by calling Fannaråkhytta.

<u>My notes</u>

I did this hike after two days of pouring rain, which meant that what would have been the straightforward trail was actually a lot of wading for me. I recommend bringing an extra snack and something warm to drink for the wait at the bottom of the glacier. I waited for close to 45 minutes before the guides arrived and started the equipment demonstration, and having an extra drink kept me from getting grouchy. I'd also put on all your extra layers if it's cloudy - it was much colder on the glacier than I expected.

Fannårken has much more limited facilities than the other DNT serviced cabins - there are no showers, no kiosk for supplies, no place to dispose of trash, and a very basic drying room. I had minimal phone service at the cabin, and there were many spots without service on the hike.

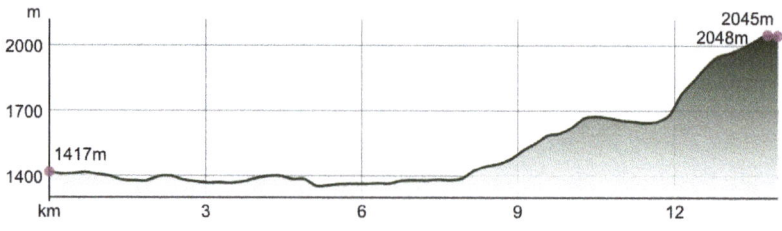

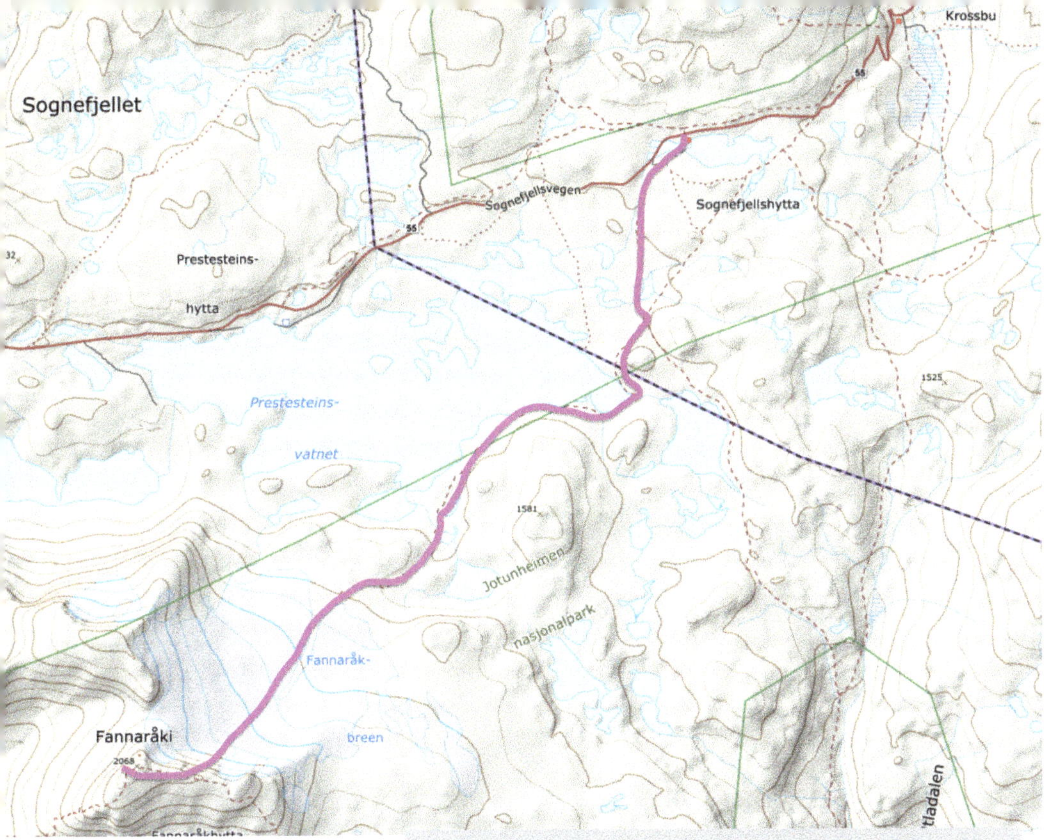

Be mentally prepared for the last two kilometers after the glacier - I wasn't. For some reason, I thought the guided section would drop me right at the cabin, and I wasn't ready for the last bit of the climb.

Sognefjellshytta to Skogadalsbøen

14.0 km
8.7 miles

226 meters
741 feet

803 meters
2,634 feet

5 hours
Challenging

Start the hike by finding the trailhead - it's at the south of the parking lot for Sognefjellshytta. From here, go about 1.5 kilometers through straightforward terrain until you reach a fork with the trail to Fannaråkhytta. Take the trail towards the east / left and continue going south. The trail goes through occasionally rocky sections, but the trail is generally easy to see and follow.

Keep going south into the Vetle Utladalen valley, dropping elevation the entire time. There are a few bridges in this section over rivers. Continue dropping through the valley until you hit about 11 kilometers in total. From here, the trail hits an intersection, with trails to Fannaråkhytta, Leirvassbu, and Turtagrø. Take the trail towards Skogadalsbøen, which goes through a flat section for another two kilometers before reaching the cabin.

The last two kilometers to Skogadalsbøen can be very wet and marshy, but there have been planks laid down to make the crossing easier.

My notes

This is an easy day in comparison to many of the other days in Jotunheimen. The trail drops elevation all day, and if the weather is clear, you get beautiful views south into the valley in front of you.

If you go the other way, it's also a straightforward trail - just budget enough time to account for the amount of climb.

Skogadalsbøen is in a bit of a forest, so you won't see the cabin until you're about a hundred meters away. Keep checking the map and you'll get there eventually

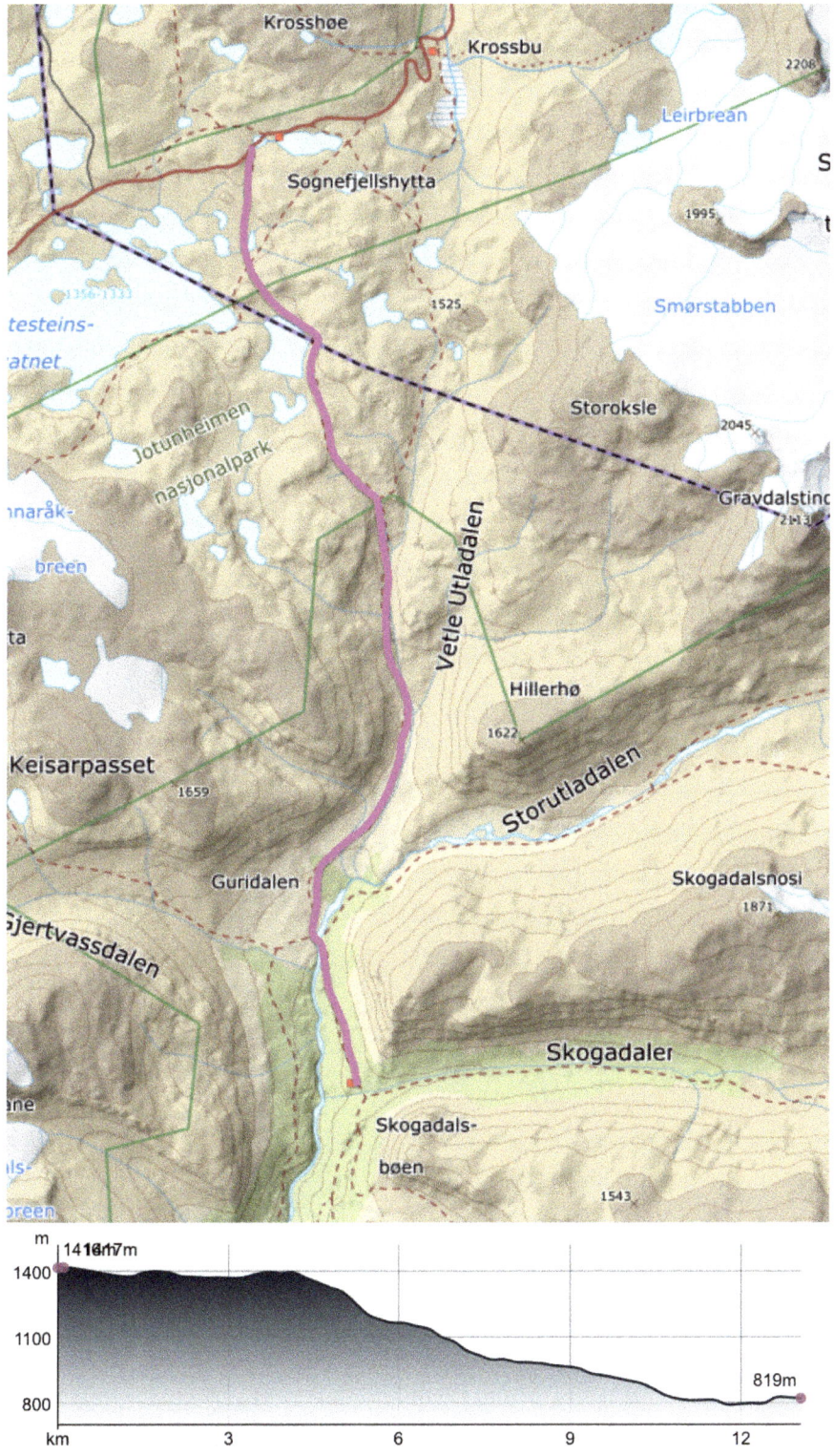

Fannaråkhytta to Skogadalsbøen

11.9 km
7.4 miles

363 meters
1,191 feet

1,217 meters
3,992 feet

6 hours
Challenging

The first part of the day is slow going as the trail goes through steep, rocky downhills, as well as snowfields. Once you pass through the rocky section and the snowfields, you enter an alpine meadow where you continue to steeply drop . Once you finish dropping down through the meadow, you'll cross a bridge, then go about a kilometer to Skogdalsbøen. This part of the trail is thankfully flat and easy to navigate.

My hiking notes

I thought that this was going to be an easy day because it was all downhill. It was not. This is a very steep descent, starting in a rocky section and then going on a dirt trail. I ended up being slower on the downhill than I was on the uphill on the previous days.

Watch out for snow bridges when you're crossing over rivers. I met someone in the cabin who'd fallen through one and was soaking wet.

2046m
2047m

2000m
1600m
1200m
815m
800m

km   2   4   6   8   10

Skogadalsbøen to Vettismorki

10.2 km
6.3 miles

551 meters
1,807 feet

700 meters
2,296 feet

5 hours
Challenging

Start the trail going south from Skogadalsbøen, following signs towards Vetti or Vettismorki. The trail is mostly flat until you cross over a bridge over the Uradøla. From here, the trail starts to climb, first in dirt and then in rocky terrain. It's four kilometers of climbing, so pace yourself. The views out into the valley are spectacular through this section, especially as you get into the rockier terrain.

At the midpoint of the trail, about 5.2 kilometers in, the trail starts to drop elevation. The way down is steeper than the way up - there's a fairly steep descent for another 2.5 kilometers before the trail flattens out slightly. The terrain is a mixture of rocky and dirt through here.

Eventually, the trail flattens out and starts to go towards Vettismorki. It can be wet through this section - watch where you're stepping. Vettismorki is in the middle of a patch of private cabins, so check the door signs to make sure you've got the right one.

My notes

Despite this trail looking like it's dropping out of the valley, there's actually quite a bit of climb involved. The high point of the trail is at almost the perfect middle of the trail. The views were much better than I expected - you're up high enough to have an overview of all of the surrounding mountains.

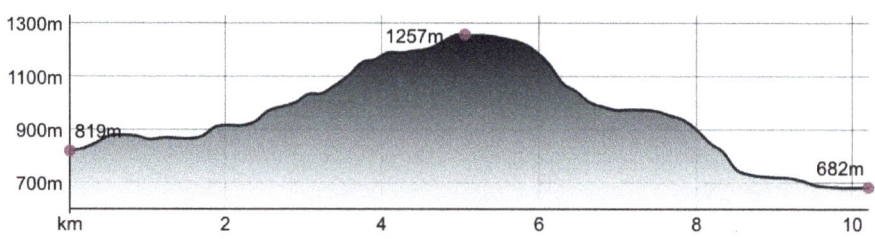

It is possible to do this as a day hike from Skogadalsbøen, going out and back to Vettismorki, but it's a very long day.

Olavsbu to Skogadalsbøen - Skogadalen

17.2 km
10.7 miles

330 meters
1,082 feet

930 meters
3,050 feet

6 hours
Challenging

There are two paths from Olavsbu to Skogadalsbøen - you can also take the route over Rauddalen and Storutladalen.

The trail starts by going northwest from Olavsbu through some rockier terrain near the cabin. Continue for about three kilometers until you reach the south side of the Rauddalsvatnet. About halfway along the Rauddalsvatnet, there's an intersection. The trail over Skogadalen turns off to the left / south, turning sharply south.

The trail climbs up and over a ridge. The elevation gain feels more intense than it looks on the map. Drop down on the south side of the ridge. The trail intersects with the trail from Gjendebu to Skogadalsbøen. Turn towards the west, going along the south side of a series of small lakes. This section can be rocky. From here, the trail continues to drop elevation, eventually entering the Skogadal valley.

There are about five kilometers in the forest before you reach the cabin - it can feel mentally longer than it looks on the map, especially at the end of a day of hiking. The trail drops directly into the cabin complex at the end of the day. You'll pass by a great place to jump into the river and go swimming next to a large bridge, about 100 meters before the cabin.

My notes

I preferred the route through the Rauddalen because it was in open mountain terrain for longer, so I felt like I had more views out onto the surrounding mountains. Both are great hikes, though.

There may be some rivers that you need to rock hop across here, especially if it's rained recently or there's a lot of snow melt.

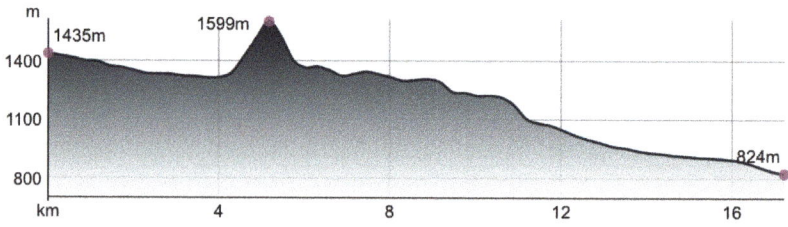

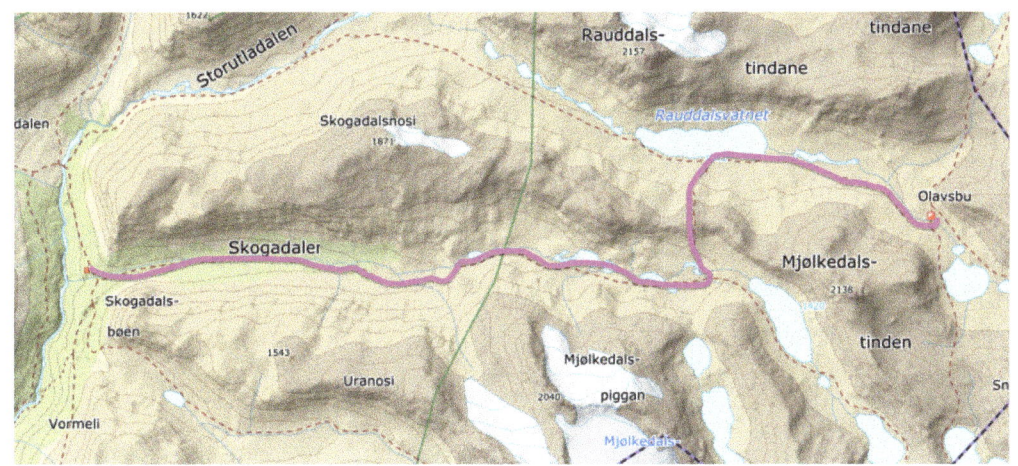

The valleys around Skogadalsbøen are generally full of plant and animal life - I hiked the whole day here listening to birds chirping and smelling wildflowers

Olavsbu to Skogadalsbøen-Rauddalen/Storutladalen

18.2 km
11.3 miles

232 meters
2,761 feet

839 meters
2,752 feet

6 hours
Challenging

This route is a gentle downhill for most of the day - and it's even in friendly terrain, so it's a good change from the more intense hikes the days before.

The trail starts by going northwest from Olavsbu through some rockier terrain near the cabin. Continue for about three kilometers until you reach the south side of the Rauddalsvatnet. From here, continue to follow the trail along the lake, continuing as the lake turns into a river. It's pretty flat through the section, although the terrain is a bit rocky.

From here, the trail starts to curve towards the west as you enter Storutladalen, a valley leading to Skogadalsbøen. The trail continues to drop elevation, with some flatter sections mixed with some steeper ones. The terrain changes into a dirt trail with plants and some small trees around you. Continue to follow the south side of the river until the trail turns towards the south.

From here, it's about 2.5 kilometers to Skogadalsbøen in a flat section through the valley.

My hiking notes

This is a really lovely hike if you've got nice weather. There were wildflowers along the trail, birds chirping, and a birch forest towards the end. The views were spectacular the whole way. There's no sections that are technically challenging, just long.

I prefer this route to the route over Skogadalen. The other route is in the forest for longer, so I didn't feel that I had the same fantastic views.

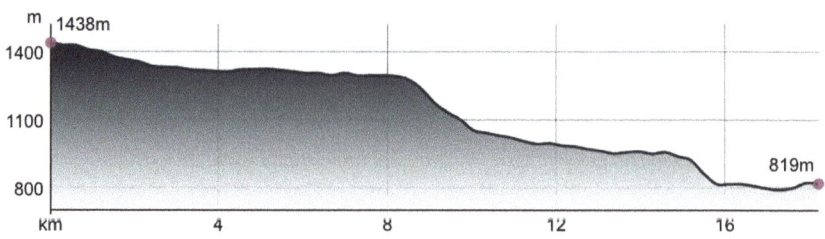

The cabin appears seemingly out of nowhere as you get closer. I kept wondering where it was and whether I really only had a few hundred meters to go, and then it just showed up.

Skogadalsbøen to Fondsbu

24.8 km
15.4 miles

1,129 meters
3,703 feet

1,015 meters
3,329 feet

6 hours
Challenging

Today starts with a climb up to Uradalsbandet, a saddle, at 1,400 meters. From here, you should have a great view towards Uranostind at 2,157 meters, assuming that it's not raining. It's a straightforward trail, dirt most of the time. After this, you'll hike along a lake with small rocks.

It's fairly flat through this section until you hit about kilometer twenty and start the drop down to Fondsbu through a meadow. The trail to Fondsbu can be a little difficult to follow, as there are private cabins around Fondsbu. I chose to drop straight down on the marked T path and then take the road to Fondsbu, but you can also take smaller, unmarked trails to Fondsbu.

My hiking notes:

The first part of the hike has a lot of plant life on it, so if it's been raining, wear rain pants or gaiters to keep water from getting into your shoes. It can be rocky after that, so be careful if there are snowfields - you don't want to fall through onto rocks.

Solbjørg Kvålshaugen, who runs Fondsbu, is a celebrity among outdoor lovers in Norway. She sings a song for all of the guests before dinner, and it's one of the highlights of staying in the cabin system. Fondsbu also had the most delicious cabbage I've ever eaten (and cabbage is not usually a food that inspires gushing praise). There are even indoor flush toilets and wifi.

If you need to get back into civilization, there is a bus during the summer from Fondsbu that connects to bus service to Oslo.

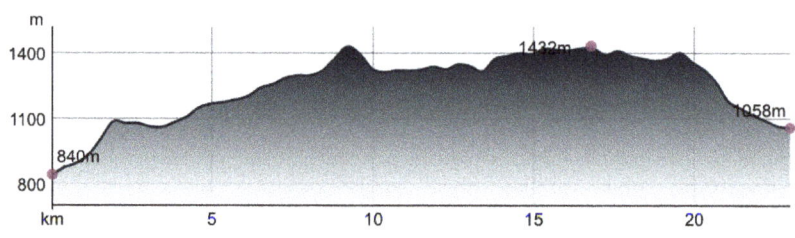

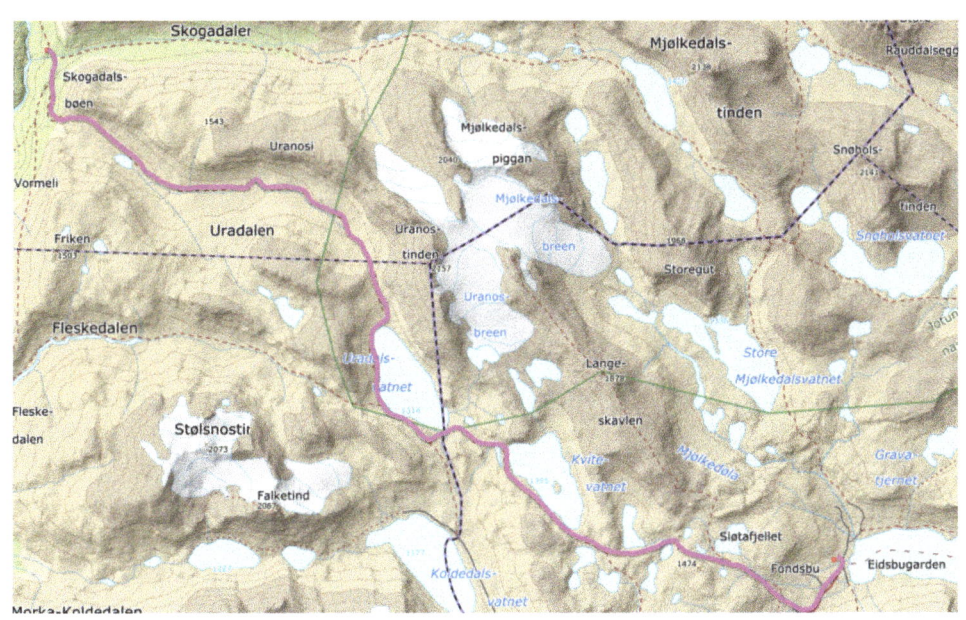

This hike is a study in contrasts - from the bright green valley near Skogadalsbøen up into the gray and slightly desolate high mountains, then back down to Fondsbu along the lake

Gjendebu to Skogadalsbøen

30.3 km	753 meters	919 meters	6 hours
18.8 miles	2,470 feet	3,014 feet	Challenging

Start from Gjendebu, going towards the southwest. Start to climb up through the Veslådalen. Cross over a summer bridge as you exit the forest, then continue to climb. At about five kilometers into the hike, the trail forks off, with the trail towards Fondsbu going towards the south, Follow the trail towards Skogadalsbøen and continue to climb.

The trail goes by several small lakes. There are a few sections where you may need to rock up across rivers and wet patches, depending on the recent weather. The terrain can be quite rocky in this section.

At about thirteen kilometers of total hiking, the trail hits both its high point and another intersection - this time intersecting with the trail that runs from Fondsbu to Olavsbu. Continue going straight and start to drop elevation. About 1.5 kilometers after the intersection, there is a river that will need to be waded across.

The trail meets up with the trail from Olavsbu to Skogadalsbøen over Skogadalen. Follow the trail as it goes along the south side of a series of small lakes. This section can be rocky. From here, the trail continues to drop elevation, eventually entering the Skogadal valley.

There are about five kilometers in the forest before you reach the cabin - it can feel mentally longer than it looks on the map, especially at the end of a day of hiking. The trail drops directly into the cabin complex at the end of the day. You'll pass by a great place to jump into the river and go swimming next to a large bridge, about 100 meters before the cabin.

My notes

This is an intense day, going more than 30 kilometers in sometimes very rocky terrain. If you're hiking in the shoulder season or not sure about it, I recommend breaking this hike up by spending the night at Olavsbu rather than attempting it in one go.

Mentally prepare yourself for the end towards Skogadalsbøen - the trail goes through the valley for a long time, and you won't be able to see the cabin. It can feel like you're not making progress and the trail never ends.

Vetle Utladalen
Hillerhø
Storutladalen
Skogadalsnosi
Skogadalen
Skogadals-
bøen
Rauddals-
tindane
Høgvagl-
tindane
Olavsbu
Mjølkedals-
tinden
Mjølkedals-
piggan
Uranosi
Uradalen
Vormeli
Fleskedalen
Storegut
Store
Rauddalseggje
Skarddalseggje
Rauddalen
tinden
Storådalen
Gjendebu
Gjende
Vesleådalen

m
1400
1100
800
km
7
14
21
28
1598m
991m
819m

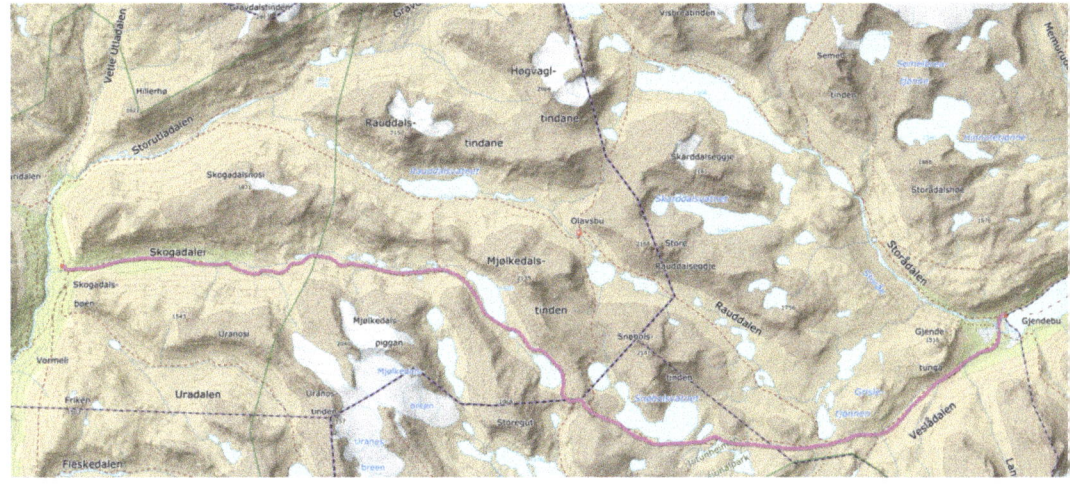

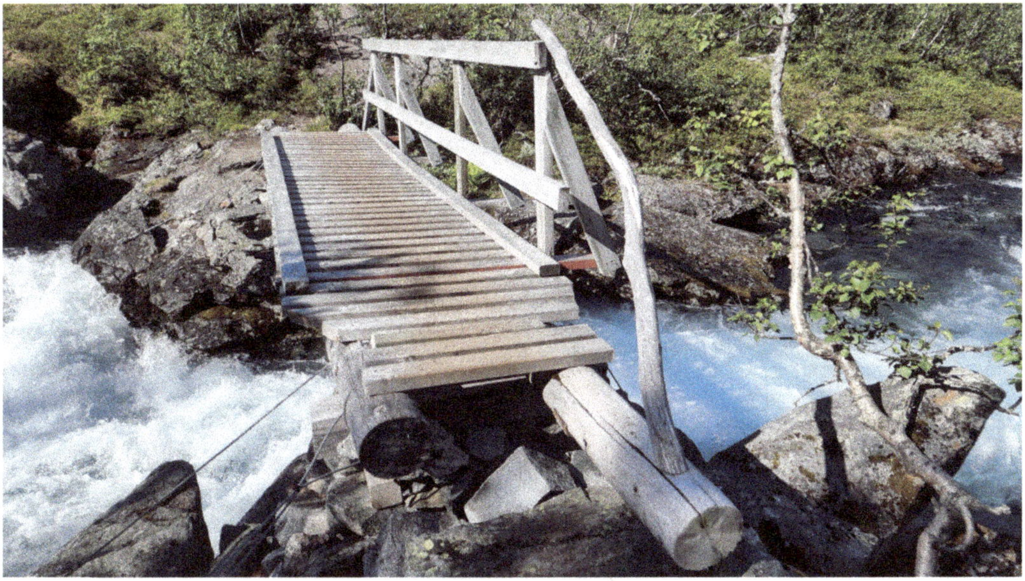

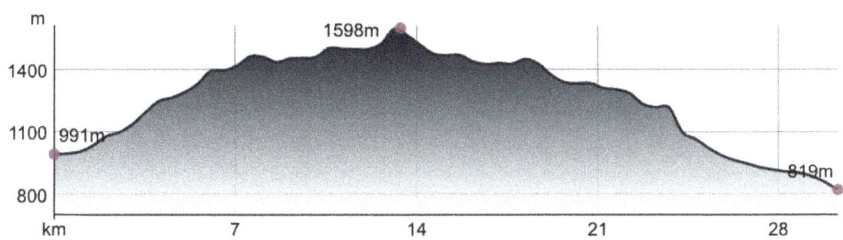

Olavsbu to Gjendebu

15.6 km
8.7 miles

77 meters
253 feet

517 meters
1,696 feet

5 hours
Challenging

Start by taking the trail towards Gjendebu (obviously) for the first 1.5 kilometers of the hike. There is an old trail on the western side of the lake - it's no longer in general use, but people will sometimes use it in case of snowfields. Ask in the cabin if you're not sure about trail conditions.

From here, the path starts to go towards the southeast through the Rauddalen valley. This section has a very gentle descent and is in lightly rocky terrain. There can be snowfields until late in the year, but it's easy to pass regardless.

After about 6.5 kilometers of total hiking, the trail starts to turn towards the east more sharply and meets up with the trail coming from Fondsbu. The trail can go through wetter sections here, particularly if it's rained recently. Follow the trail for another five kilometers into Gjendebu, crossing over a bridge when you're directly in front of the cabin.

My notes

This is a relaxed hike with gentle descent throughout the day. There are no steep sections or drop offs, but be aware that there can be snowfields until late in the season. There are plenty of spots to fill up your water bottle during the day as well, since the trail is almost always next to a lake or a river.

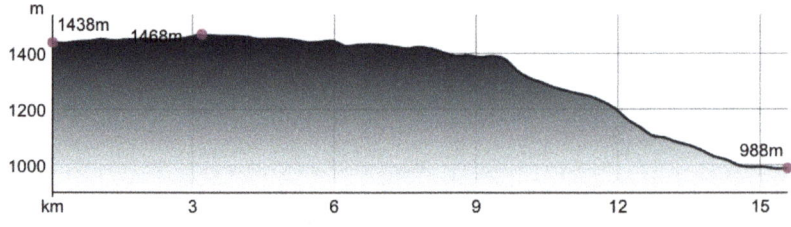

Olavsbu is DNT Oslo's largest self-service cabin, and it can get very busy during the summers. About half of the beds are available for pre-booking, which I recommend if you're traveling with a large group

Olavsbu to Fondsbu

13.8 km
8.6 miles

335 meters
1,099 feet

716 meters
2,348 feet

6 hours
Challenging

Start by taking the trail towards Gjendebu for the first 1.5 kilometers of the hike. There is an old trail on the western side of the lake - it's no longer in general use, but people will sometimes use it in case of snowfields. At about 1.5 kilometers in, cross in between two lakes and then start to take the trail towards the south. This section is flat and easy to hike.

From here, there's a short climb over a saddle, then a gradual drop down between Mjølkedalstinden and Snøhøltinden, two peaks ("-tinden" means "the peak"). Continue going south along the trail and pass the trails going to Gjendebu and Skogadalsbøen. From here, it's a steep descent down until you reach the cabins around Fondsbu. You can decide whether to take the road or one of the trails through the cabins to reach Fondsbu at the edge of the lake.

My notes

This is a really beautiful way to get from Olavsbu to Fondsbu - while it's long, I didn't think that it was overly difficult. There can be snowfields here until late in the summer, so I recommend bringing poles.

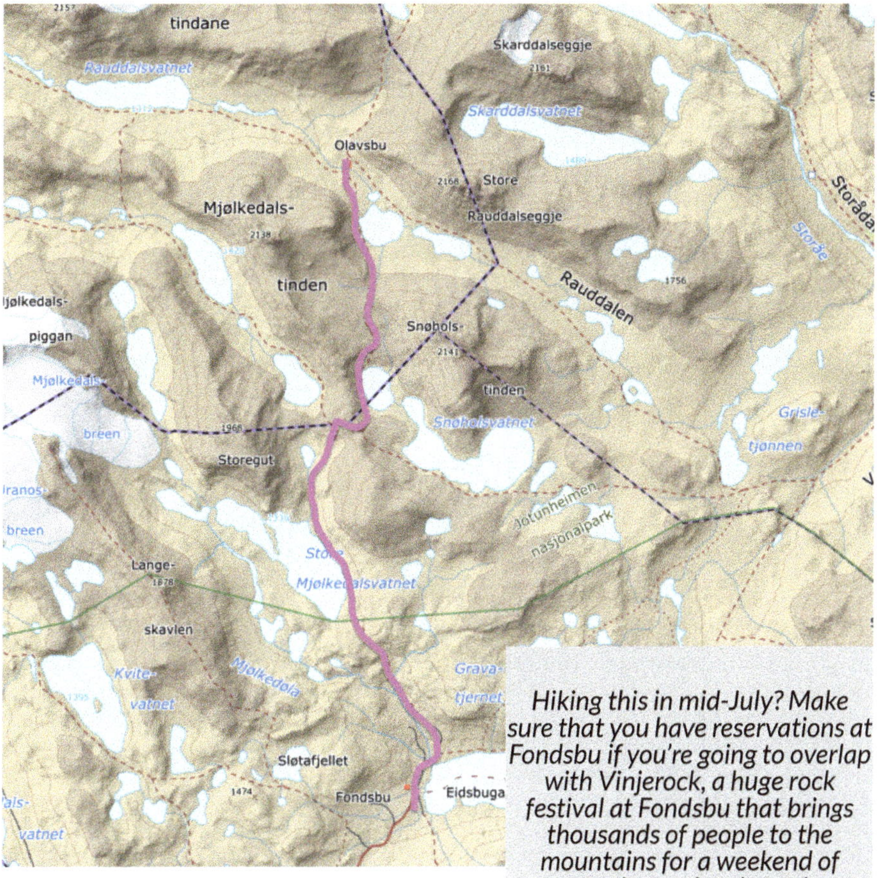

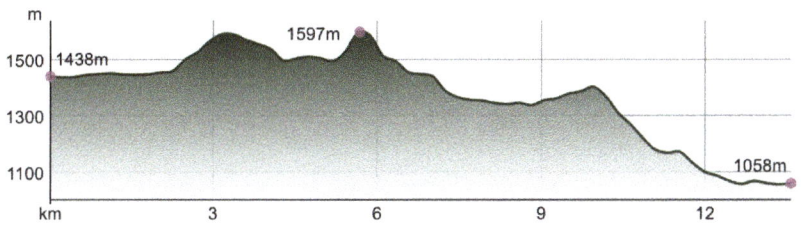

Hiking this in mid-July? Make sure that you have reservations at Fondsbu if you're going to overlap with Vinjerock, a huge rock festival at Fondsbu that brings thousands of people to the mountains for a weekend of camping and rock music

Vettismorki to Tyinholmen

22.3 km
13.8 miles

1,061 meters
3,480 feet

654 meters
2,145 feet

8 hours
Challenging

This is a long and demanding trail. Start by going south from Vettismokri in sometimes wet terrain. Within the first kilometer, start a steep climb up towards the Hjelledalen valley. When you reach the valley, turn towards the east and continue to climb more gently along the north side of the river. The terrain will become increasingly rocky through this section.

At about 10.5 kilometers of total hiking, the trail reaches the end of the Hjellevatnet lake. Go around the north side of the lake, then turn towards the south. The trail crosses over the river into the lake here - note that this may require wading and can be quite difficult to cross if there's high water levels. Cross the river and continue to climb through rocky terrain for another 2.5 kilometers.

From here, it's relatively flat until you round Breikvamsnosi and then start the steep drop towards Tyinholmen. Note that this trail is less well marked than many of the other Jotunheimen trails - the cairns are spread further apart from each other than normal.

Drop down and meet a construction road that you take to Tyinholmen. From here, you'll have to go along the road or catch the bus to get from Tyinholmen to Fondsbu. It's an additional 4 kilometers at the end of the day, but it's fast.

My notes

I'd recommend going over Skogadalsbøen if you have the time to do it - it makes the day more manageable, and I love the trail from Vettismorki to Skogadalsbøen. That route also avoids the potentially difficult river crossings on this route.

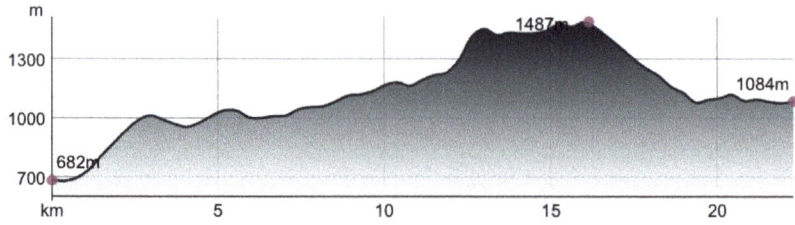

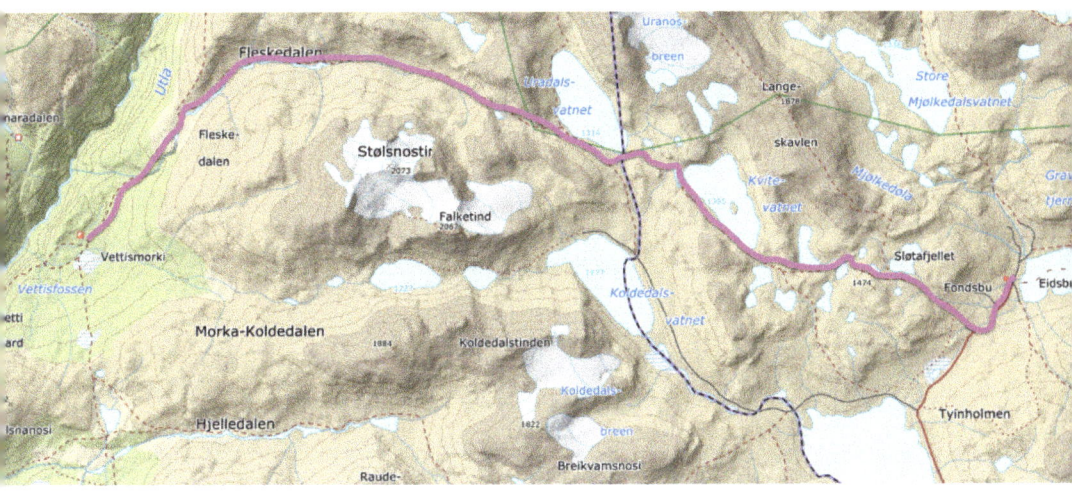

This is a spectacular hike, but it's very long - leave early from Vettismorki. The later part of the day can be rocky and slow going, and the first part of the day has friendly trails but a tough climb

Fondsbu to Yksendalsbu

15.9 km
9.9 miles

747 meters
2,450 feet

745 meters
2,444 feet

6 hours
Challenging

Start by heading southeast from Fondsbu. The trail climbs up about 300 meters of elevation in the first three to four kilometers, so pace yourself through this section. It is also quite rocky for the first half of the day.

After climbing, the trail flattens out slightly and starts to pass by a number of small lakes. Gently drop elevation until you pass Dryllin lake at about 8.5 kilometers of total hiking. From here, there's a steep drop into the Vølodalen valley, and then a climb up onto the other side of the Vølodalen valley. From here, the trail drops steeply to Yksendalsbu.

Note that it can be tough to see the trail during the drop into Yksendalsbu - there is fast growing vegetation here that can be quite difficult to see though.

My notes

This is definitely a hike that requires a climb up and then a climb down, but the views are worth it. I recommend booking ahead at Yksendalsbu if it's a busy time of year, because it's a very small cabin.

I skied this and loved it, but the ski tracks are different than the hiking tracks here. It avoids the steep drop down to Yksendalsbu, since that's avalanche prone terrain.

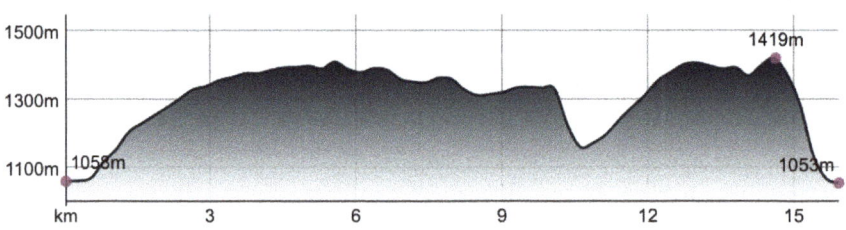

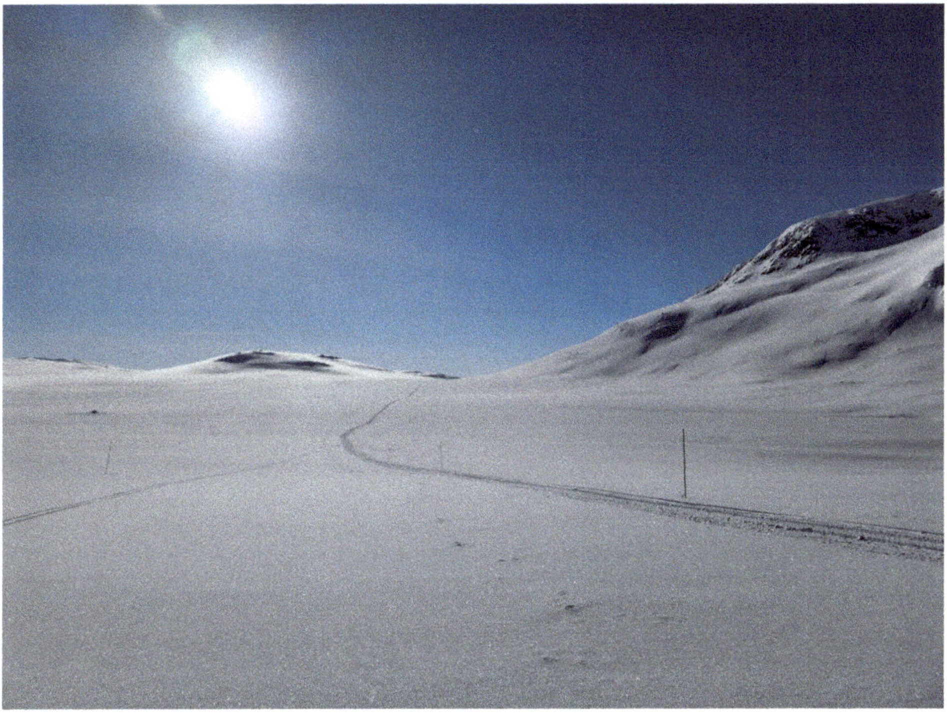

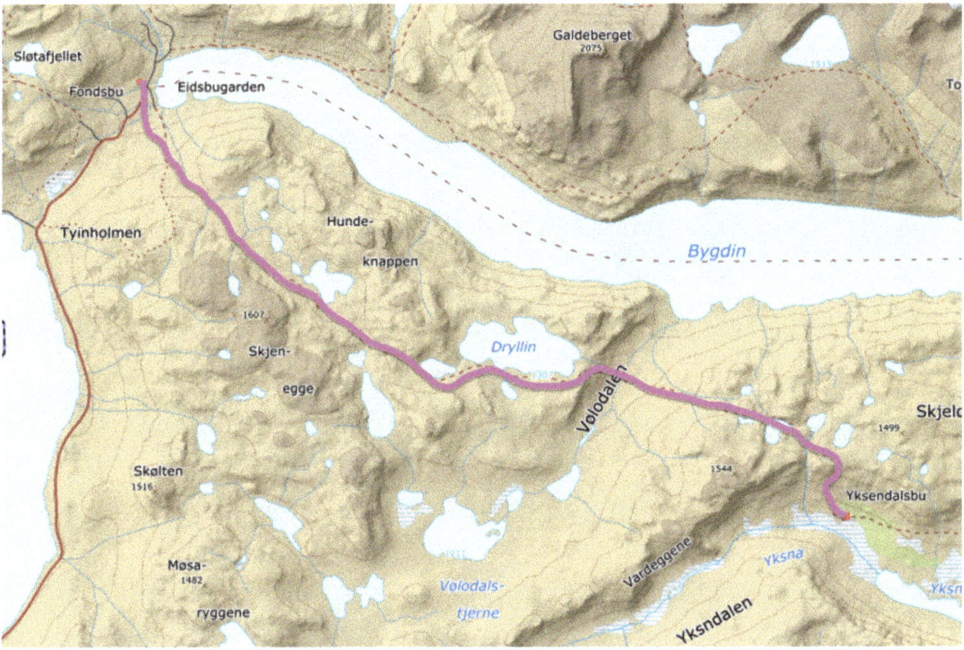
Sløtafjellet
Fondsbu
Eidsbugarden
Galdeberget
2075
Tyinholmen
Hunde-
knappen
Bygdin
1607
Skjen-
egge
Dryllin
Vølodalen
1499
1544
Yksendalsbu
Skølten
1516
Møsa-
1482
ryggene
Vølodals-
tjerne
Vardeggene
Yksna
Yksndalen

Fondsbu to Slettningsbu

22.5 km
14.0 miles

684 meters
2,244 feet

430 meters
1,410 feet

6 hours
Challenging

From Fondsbu, you start today's hike following the road to Tyinholmen. Pass Tyinholmen after about three kilometers of hiking and continue along the road for a few hundred meters, then turn off to the west as the road starts to gain elevation. You'll continue to follow this trail until you get to a flat section along the edge of Tyin lake.

This section is easy in dry weather, but very wet in damp weather - I needed to test every step to make sure I wasn't stepping into a puddle. After the lake, you'll reach the Fv53 road, which you'll walk along for a kilometer before turning left (towards the south) and walking up through a small collection of cabins. It's a little bit difficult to find the trail through here, so check UT frequently.

From here, it's three kilometers of climb in gentle terrain until you reach Slettningsbu along the Øvre Årdalsvatnet lake at 1,313 meters above sea level.

My hiking notes

I thought this would be a relatively easy day because of the elevation profile and distance, but I again underestimated the weather. The morning is a little bit boring as you go along the road to Tyin. Once you're on the trail, it's either swampy or lovely, just depending on how much rain there's been recently. I had swampy, and I was very thankful to get to Slettningsbu.

Slettningsbu doesn't have a drying room or showers, since it's a self-service cabin, but others in the cabin jumped in the lake to wash off. There are also

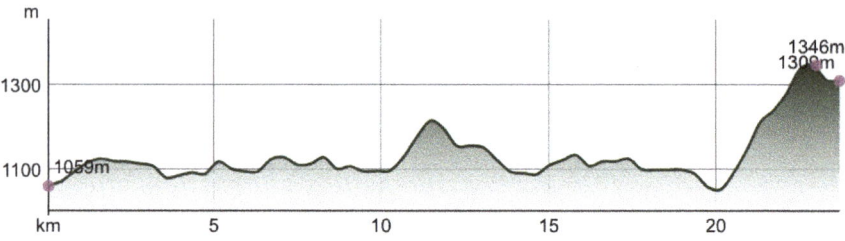

This hike takes you from Fondsbu in Jotunheimen to Slettningsbu in Skarvheimen, connecting you into the route network as it goes further south

Yksendalsbu to Tomashellern

| 11.3 km | 675 meters | 233 meters | 5 hours |
| 7.0 miles | 2,214 feet | 764 feet | Challenging |

Start by following the trail towards Bygdin for about 2.5 kilometers. The terrain can be a little bit wet, especially if it's rained recently. After 2.5 kilometers, the trail towards Tomashellern turns off towards the south.

The trail drops elevation for another kilometer, then crosses over a bridge and starts the climb up through the Dingledalen. It's a gradual climb for three more kilometers (to about seven kilometers into the hike), then a much steeper climb. The terrain is quite rocky through this section, and there are parts where it may be difficult to see the train. Follow the cairns. Eventually, the trail flattens out and goes over a rocky but flat section for about two kilometers before reaching the cabin.

There are a couple of rivers near the cabin, but they're generally easy to cross by rock hopping. Unless there's very high snow melt or precipitation, they shouldn't need to be waded.

My notes

Note that this route has changed relatively recently, so not all paper maps may be accurate. Use the UT app for the latest routing, and follow the cairns rather than relying on old maps.

Tomashellern is a very cute cabin that really feels like it's in the middle of nowhere. There's no phone service, so check messages before you go. I saw one of the most beautiful sunsets of my life while skiing this section.

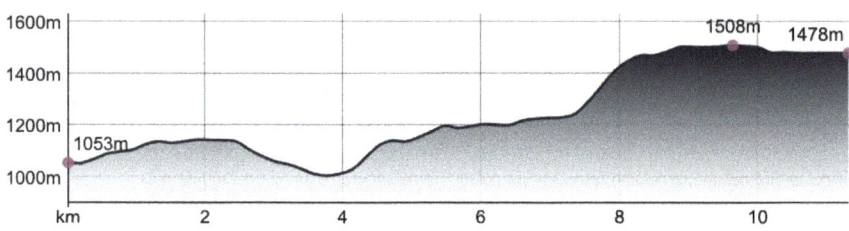

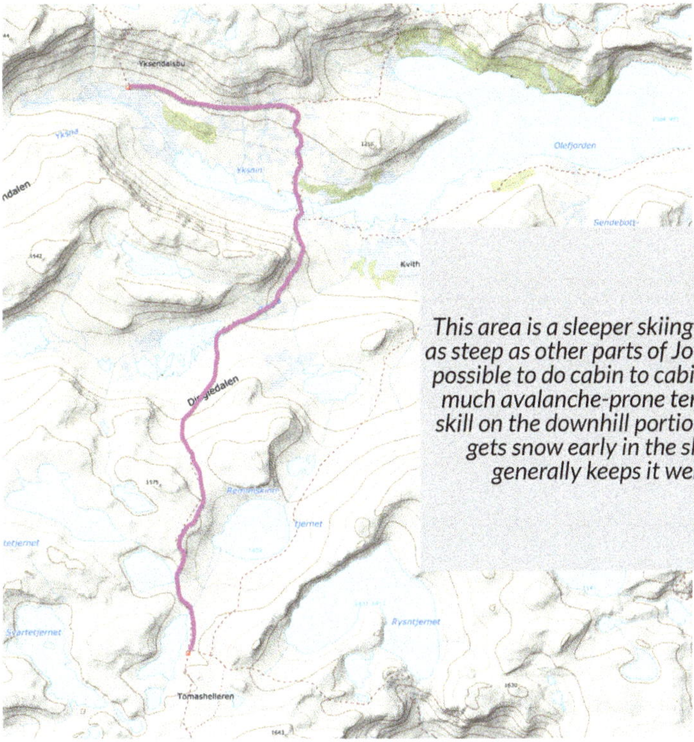

This area is a sleeper skiing hotspot - it's not as steep as other parts of Jotunheimen, so it's possible to do cabin to cabin skis without as much avalanche-prone terrain or as much skill on the downhill portions. Jotunheimen gets snow early in the ski season and generally keeps it well into May

Bygdin to Yksendalsbu

19.5 km
12.1 miles

671 meters
2,201 feet

671 meters
2,201 feet

6 hours
Challenging

This is one of the ways to get into Jotunheimen and onto the route network within the park - the bus to Beitostølen stops at Bygdin, as does the boat to and from Fondsbu.

The first kilometer of this hike goes along the road to the south of Bygdin. At the parking lot south of Bygdin, the trail leaves the road and starts to go along the south side of the Bygdin lake. Keep following this trail as it turns to the southwest and then the west - don't take the trail that goes up to the Bitihorn summit.

The first seven kilometers are mostly flat and through a combination of dirt and wet trails, with some small rocks. After seven kilometers, The trail starts a very steep climb up to the Marabotthornet at 1,376 meters. The views in this part are fantastic.

From here, continue along the top of the mountain for about 3.5 kilometers, passing by three lakes. This section is again mostly flat, with small ups and downs.

After this, at about 13 kilometers in, the trail starts to very sharply drop elevation and go down towards the Olefjorden. This section can be difficult to find the trail in, since many of the plants in the area grow quickly. I recommend long pants to avoid getting scraped up by overgrowth. After the drop, the trail turns towards the west and goes on a gentler, more clearly marked trail towards Yksendalsbu.

My notes

This is a less traveled alternative to hiking over Torfinnsbu on the way from Bygdin to Fondsbu. Yksendalsbu is a tiny cabin with eight beds in a central sleeping area, so book ahead if you're more than one or two people.

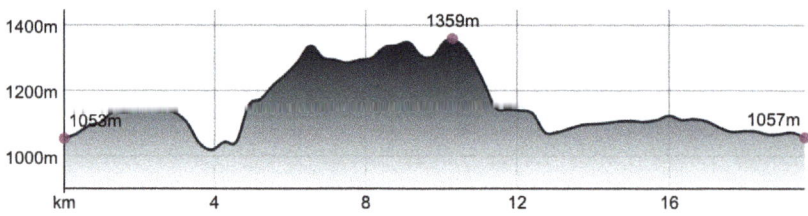

This is a less visited part of Jotunheimen, both during the summer hiking season and during the winter ski season. If you're looking for Jotunheimen's views off the beaten path, this is a great option

Fondsbu to Torfinnsbu

20.3 km
12.6 miles

749 meters
2,457 feet

748 meters
2,453 feet

8 hours
Challenging

The first part of the trail goes along the edge of the Bygdin lake, with views onto the lake and the mountains on the other side. When you've gone about 4km in total, the trail hits a crossroad with the paths towards Torfinnsbu and Gjendebu.

Note that there's a bridge in this section that's been taken down, a bridge called Nedre Høystaka. It may still be on paper maps, but use the higher up bridge, Øvre Høystaka.

From here, follow the path towards Torfinnsbu. The path quickly starts to climb, gaining elevation as it goes up towards Langedalstjernet. Once you hit the lake, you've reached the high point of the hike. The trail turns towards the southeast, then starts a sometimes steep decline down back towards the side of the Bygdin lake.

As you drop elevation, you'll cross over a few small summer bridges. If you're early in the season, you may have to do a little rock hopping or wading. With about a kilometer left in the hike, the trail starts to go along the side of the lake again and into Torfinnsbu.

My notes

You can choose to use the M/S Bitihorn rather than hiking this section if you're doing a multiday hike and want a rest day.

Torfinnsbu is a great cabin - it's right on the edge of the lake, and it's quite large. It's a popular skiing destination as well as a hiking destination - in the winters you can ski along the lake from Fondsbu or Bygdin to it.

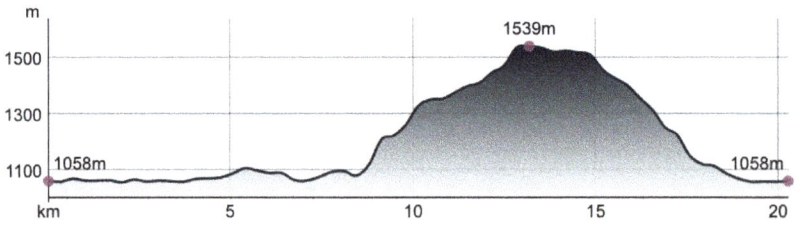

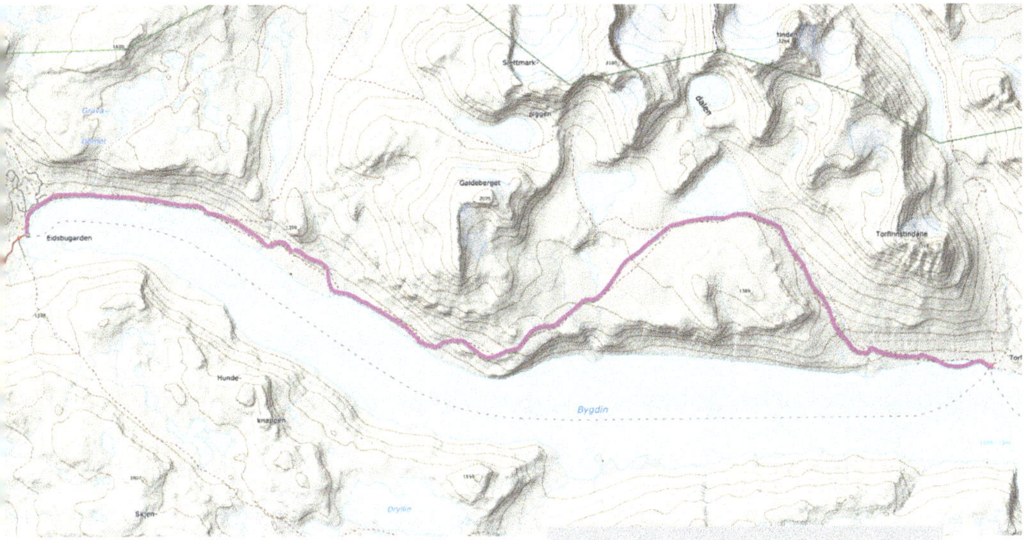

Below: one of my favorite times of day while skiing Jotunheimen was in the mornings and evenings, where you could see the light from sunrise or sunrise mixing with the fog on the frozen lakes

Bygdin to Torfinnsbu

14.0 km
8.7 miles

113 meters
371 feet

113 meters
371 feet

3.5 hours
Moderate

This is a very straightforward hike. You'll go along the side of the Bygdin lake for the entire day until you reach Torfinnsbu. There are a few places where rivers come into the lake, and there are bridges put up every summer for those crossings.

My notes

If you want, you can also take the boat from Bygdin to Torfinnsbu rather than hike this - there's also luggage transport available. This is a good warm up if you are heading out on a longer trip, or if you want to test out cabin to cabin hiking.

I actually enjoyed skiing this more than hiking it - the ski trail is in the middle of the lake, with views onto the mountains on both sides, and it's wonderfully flat.

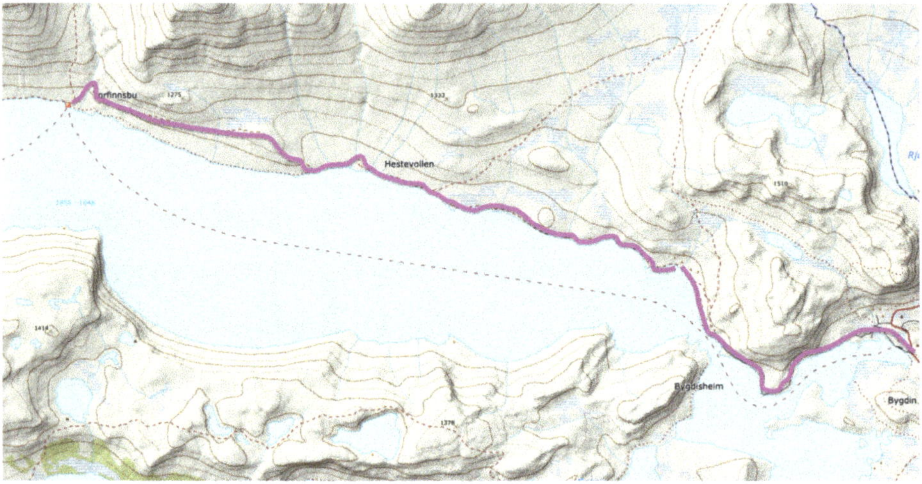

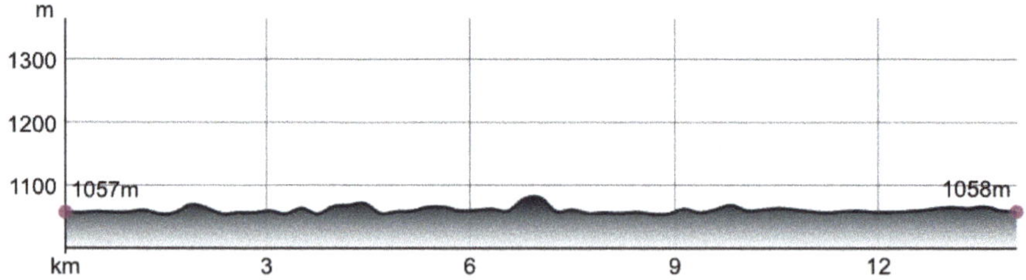

Above: Fancy bathroom art in the
outhouses at Torfinnsbu
Below: the view from ski season,
heading from Bygdin to Torfinnsbu

Torfinnsbu to Gjendebu

14.1 km
8.8 miles

493 meters
1,617 feet

553 meters
1,814 feet

5 hours
Moderate

Start by heading north from Torfinnsbu, going along the west side of the river. Start to climb up - the first kilometer is the steepest and most intense, and the climb is much more moderate for the three kilometers after that.

Cross over the river and then start to go along the east side of a series of lakes and rivers. It's largely flat for the next five kilometers after the climb.

At kilometer 9, the trail starts a steep descent into Gjendebu. This section can be quite challenging if it's rained recently or it's generally slippery. Eventually, it drops into the valley near Gjendebu. This section is much friendlier and flatter than the descent.

My notes

This is a straightforward route that starts climbing up from Torfinnsbu, then goes over a long, flat section before steeply dropping down to Gjendebu. It goes through the Svartdalen, a valley that lies at 1,500 meters above sea level. Both sides of the valley are flanked by peaks of more than 2,000 meters, so if you've got the energy, you can add some summit tours.

If you're lucky, you'll get flowers in the valley on both ends. Take it slowly on the drop down to Gjendebu, and don't assume that you'll make up any time on the descent. It's just as challenging as the ascent.

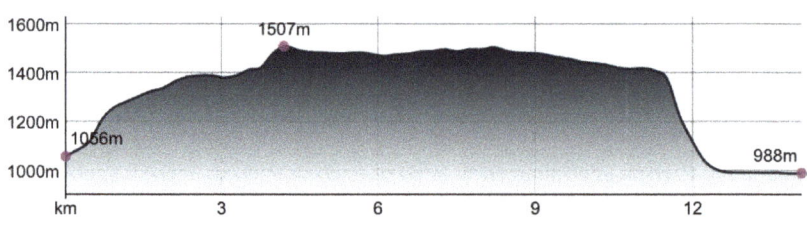

Gjendebu was voted the most romantic serviced cabin in the DNT system. There have been a lot of upgrades to the cabin in the last few years, including new furniture, showers, and upgraded bedrooms

Fondsbu to Gjendebu

15.9 km
9.9 miles

466 meters
1,528 feet

526 meters
1,725 feet

5.5 hours
Challenging

Start by going north from Fondsbu towards the road towards Olavsbu. At the fork, stay to the right and go east along the north side of the lake for about four kilometers. After this, the trail starts to climb steeply up along the side of the mountain, eventually crossing a summer bridge over Høystakka.

After crossing the bridge, the terrain noticeably flattens out, although it continues to climb. From here, the path goes through easy to pass areas, although it can be wet if it's rained recently or there's a lot of snow melt.

At about nine kilometers in, the path will start to drop towards Gjendebu. The path is mostly on dirt trails with a few rocks, but it's much easier to pass than many of the other, rocky trails in the area. Drop through the Veslådalen valley down to Gjendebu.

My notes

My experience hiking this trail was a little bit different because there were still tons of snowfields left during my hike - I didn't benefit from what were supposedly lovely and soft trails under me.

Gjendebu doesn't have phone service, so screenshot the weather and send messages in the first half of the day.

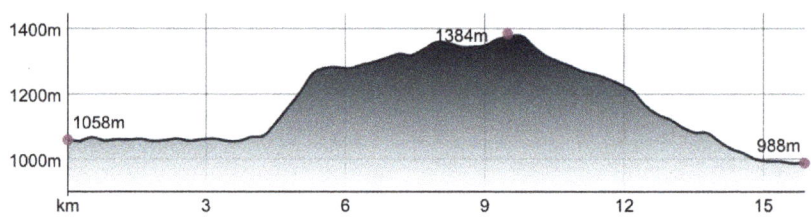

My favorite photo of Fondsbu: after a long day of hiking, a rainbow appeared over the cabin as I hiked in

Vettismorki to Hjelle

2.7 km
1.7 miles

77 meters
252 feet

464 meters
1,521 feet

4 hours
Moderate

From Vettismorki, follow signs to Vettisfossen, one of Norway's most famous waterfalls. It's only 1.2 kilometers to the waterfall on friendly trails, so you can even incorporate it with the day before if you're feeling good.

Stop and admire the waterfall. After that, the trail drops steeply through the forest until you reach Vetti Gard, a historic farming complex. Once you pass Vetti Gard, the trail continues to drop steeply for another hundred meters of elevation before flattening out a bit. From here, start going along a farm road towards Hjelle, which is a large parking lot for people going for hikes in the area.

During the summers, there's a morning bus that takes hikers from Hjelle to Øvre Årdal or Turtagrø. If there's no bus, just keep following the road until you reach Øvre Årdal (or until you can convince a cabin friend to give you a ride).

My hiking notes

Vettisfossen is really impressive - there's a viewing platform so that you can appreciate how big it actually is. If you're not going all the way to Øvre Årdal, it's worth making the detour from Vettismorki.

The end of the day here is a little bit boring along the road. If there are other hikers, you might be able to catch a ride with them.

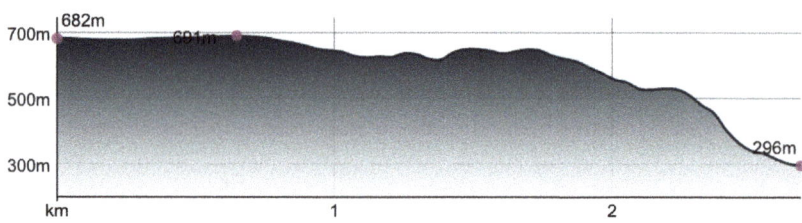

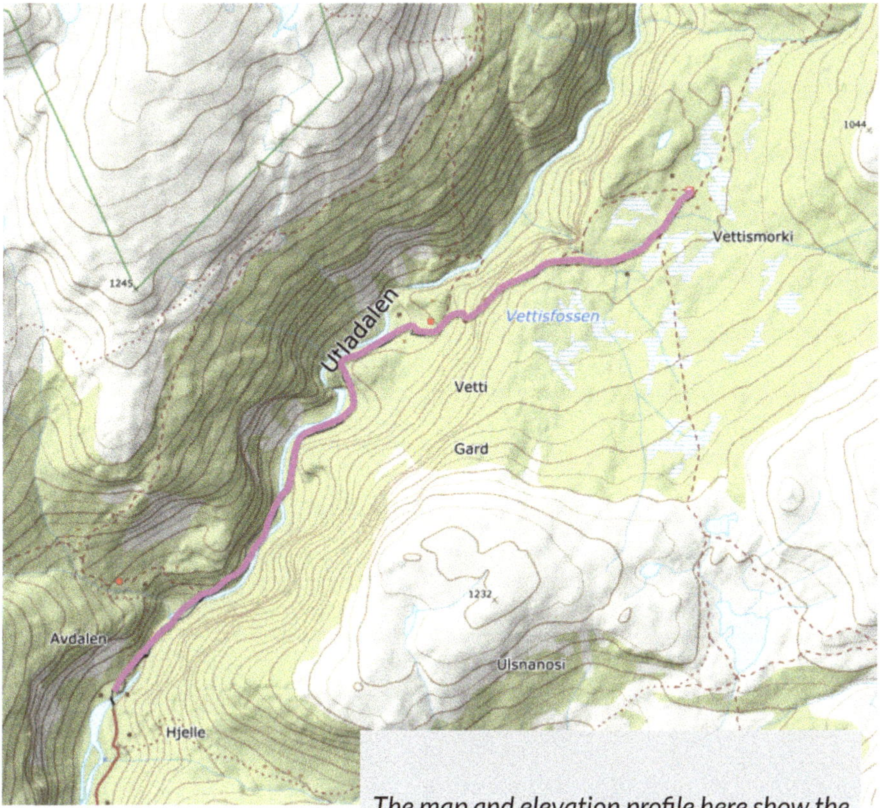

The map and elevation profile here show the distance to Hjelle. It's an additional 6-8 kilometers on the road back to Øvre Årdal

Knutshøe

12.5 km
7.8 miles

680 meters
2,230 feet

680 meters
2,230 feet

6 hours
Challenging

Start at the parking lot or trailhead along Valdresflyvegen. From here, cross the river Varga. There's a clearly marked path that goes through a bit of a valley before beginning the climb up towards Knutshøe. Within the first two kilometers, there's the first climbing section. You may need to wait for others to climb up before you scramble up this section.

After that, the trail continues to climb. There are a few sections with a steep drop off, so watch your footing. Continue to climb up until you reach the ridge. Here, the trail flattens out and becomes much easier to walk. Go over the ridge, then down the western side of the ridge. There are no shortcuts back - once you reach the ridge, you'll need to walk along the entire ridge before dropping down.

The trail down into the valley is mostly dirt. From here, it's an easy trail past a lake that's great for bathing on hot days. Follow the trail as it goes along the southern end of Knutshøe and back to the start point.

My hiking notes

Knutshøe is an alternative hike to Besseggen - although I think it's better to do them both, and I'd pick Besseggen if you have to choose. It's a great hike because you get views into Jotunheimen and Besseggen, and it's a bit less crowded than Besseggen.

It's technically a little bit easier than Besseggen, with a little bit less elevation gain and a shorter climbing section, but it's still not super easy. There are two steep sections, one towards the beginning of the climb and one at the end, that can be a little bit scary if you're afraid of heights. Similar to Besseggen, I wouldn't recommend it in the rain.

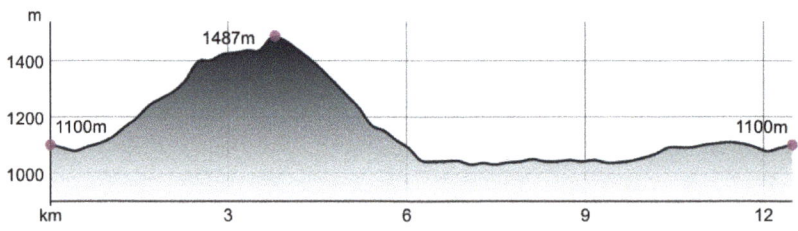

There are certainly some steep drop offs on this one - Knutshøe is slightly easier than Besseggen, but still a tough hike.

Logistics

Getting There and Back

Jotunheimen is one of the easiest parks to get to and from. From Otta and Lom, there are multiple buses each day to Gjendesheim and Bygdin. From Oslo and Bergen, there are buses directly to the major cabins.

- **Bygdin:** the line NW161 Valdresekspressen goes from Oslo to Bygdin, Beitostølen, and Gjendesheim during peak season. Departures up to three times a day.

- **Fondsbu:** line 300 goes from Eidsbugarden next to Fondsbu to Tyinkrysset, where you can then transfer to buses that go to Oslo and Bergen. The bus runs twice a day. You can also take the boat, M/S Bitihorn, to Bygdin.

- **Gjendebu**: the Gjendebåten (Gjende boat) has regularly scheduled service back to Gjendesheim, corresponding with the bus to Oslo.

- **Gjendesheim:** Gjendesheim has regular bus service to Oslo and fairly frequent bus service to Lom when the road is open (e.g. not during parts of the winters). Tickets to Oslo need to be booked in advance, while tickets to Lom do not.

- **Leirvassbu:** bus line 203 goes twice daily during peak hiking season. It goes from Leirvassbu to Lom, where you can catch connections back to the rest of Norway.

- **Sognefjellshytta:** buses to Sogndal / Lom (line 200) and Fortun / Gaupne (line 860) stop by the cabin once or twice a day. From Sogndal, you can fly to Bergen or Oslo. From Lom, there's bus service to either Oslo or Lillehammer.

- **Spiterstulen**: line 201 goes from Spiterstulen to Lom twice daily during peak hiking season. Lom has a variety of bus connections to other destinations in Norway.

- **Vettismorki:** from Vettismorki, you can hike down to Øvre Årdal or Hjelle. From here, you can take the bus to Lom or Sogndal to catch transport back to Oslo and Bergen.

I recommend booking tickets on the boat in advance - they have a limited number of seats, and they can sell out during peak times. You can book online and get a ticket with a QR code. If you haven't booked online (or haven't had phone service at Gjendebu), you can also pay at the gate subject to availability.

Luggage Transport

You're in luck if you're looking for luggage transport - Jotunheimen is one of only two areas where you can have your baggage transported during your hike. There are boats that run from Gjendesheim to Gjendebu and from Bygdin to Fondsbu, and it's possible to book a spot for your bag on those boats.

Supplies

If you're planning to camp, bring the food that you need with you. There are places to buy supplies in all of the serviced cabins, but they are generally small kiosks that only sell snacks and a couple of varieties of freeze-dried food.

For other small needs, like band-aids or chocolate, you can purchase what you need at the serviced cabins and hotels.

You can rent hiking shoes and a jacket at Gjendesheim if you're planning to only do a couple of days. If you want to purchase hiking gear, take the bus to Lom or Vagå from the park and use one of the sporting goods stores there.

Timing

The best time to go hiking is from July to early September. If you go in June, you may run into a few spots where the summer bridges haven't been put out yet - summer bridges are temporary bridges that DNT volunteers put out in mid to late June. You will also hit snowfields.

There is a music festival, Vinjerock, at Fondsbu during mid-July. That brings a few thousand people into the area around Fondsbu, so I recommend avoiding it if you're looking to be hiking instead.

If you're skiing, March and April are generally the best months. You will usually have snow until May, but some of the lower areas may start to be bare. The cabins are all open starting in mid to late March through at least Easter.

Every year is slightly different - check SeNorge.no for the latest snow depth and weather conditions.

Camping

Norway has some of the most permissive laws in the world around camping. Norway has a law called the Allemannsretten that guarantees the ability of people to explore and experience nature, even in privately owned areas, as long as you're in uncultivated land. Once you're in the wilderness, you may camp in any area, as long as you're at least 150 meters away from the nearest inhabited house or cabin.

Note that the 150 meters applies to the DNT cabins as well - most serviced cabins have marked areas where you can camp, and you'll have to pay a small fee to use the toilets or other common facilities.

Campfires are prohibited everywhere in Norway from April 15 to September 15, except in specifically marked areas in camping sites and by the coast. You will need to bring a gas stove to cook, and in the case of drought, even gas stoves may be banned.

Winter Considerations

Can you ski Jotunheimen? Absolutely!

If you're experienced with randonee skis, there is a route called the Jotunheimen Haute Route, which is a Norwegian equivalent to the Alpine haute route. It skis over Norway's two highest peaks, Glittertinden and Galdhøpiggen, among others.

If you're looking for something that's a bit easier, you can also replicate almost all of the summer routes in the winter. There are changes to the exact routes to avoid areas of high avalanche danger and a few that aren't recommended given avalanche danger. The trails are not groomed, so you'll need fjellski, which are a cross between Nordic and downhill backcountry skis.

I don't provide any suggested routes here because there can be major changes in routes from year to year - for example, in 2025, Gjende lake did not freeze enough for ski trips over it, and some of the cabins did not open due to lack of snow. You'll need to check ut.no or reach out to DNT for updates for the winter you plan to go.

The trails in Jotunheimen are generally marked, or kvistet, in mid-March. The exact date each year depends on snow conditions and when the cabins are opening. Check UT.no for the most recent updates.

Before planning any ski tours, make sure that you're comfortable on fjellski, or Norwegian backcountry skis, and that you have sufficient knowledge of avalanche terrain and winter safety. The trails in Jotunheimen are not groomed trails, and you will need to be prepared to navigate with compass and spend the night outside if necessary.

Planning Resources

UT App and Checking In

You can check in on the UT app (which is sometimes referred to as "SjekkUT", or "check out") at the various cabins or landmarks that you stop at. The UT app only has instructions in Norwegian, so how to do that:

Following a hike – needs to be done in advance:

1. For starters, download the ut app. Once you've downloaded the app, make a profile with your email address and log in on your device.

2. From there, you have to follow the hikes that you want to take. Following the hikes will download the maps around the cabins or areas on that hike, so you'll be able to use them without internet service. This is important.

3. Adding the route to your account is not entirely intuitive. You will need to search for the name of the hike in the search bar. From here, the critical thing is that you follow the list, not the hike. It will be at the bottom of the search results.

4. Click on the list. Make sure it's the one with the list icon. If you click the three dots on the side, you'll get a button that says "Følge", or "follow." Click on that.

5. Congratulations! You have now followed the hike. The maps will download to your phone while you have service.

Checking in:

When you get to a cabin or landmark, you can check in. Click on the icon for the cabin or landmark on the map, and a little green button that says "SjekkUT" will show up on the bottom left. Click on it.

A new screen will pop up. Click on the green button at the bottom again. If you see a screen with confetti, you're checked in!

yr.no is the best resource for weather in Norway. It allows you to hike by specific cabin or mountaintop, with the weather for that particular point rather than the overall area. It's available in English.

Senorge.no shows the current and historic weather conditions for any point in Norway. It's very useful for checking the amount of snow remaining for summer hikes, as well as seeing if it's rained recently.

ut.no is an app and website with detailed maps of Norway with the cabins and trails marked. It's unfortunately only in Norwegian, but is the best source of information on cabins and trails. You can download offline maps by going to "Profil" and then "Mine offline-kart" on the app.

Varsom.no is key for the winter and shows storm and avalanche warnings. It's available in English.

If you're stopping by a DNT office before going hiking, you can pick up a planleggingskart, or planning map. These aren't usable for hiking but are great for planning, since they show the locations of cabins and DNT cabins.

The weather can be variable in Jotunheimen based on the elevation you're at, so I recommend using YR to specifically look up the weather by cabin or mountaintop.

Packing List - Summer

In total, the gear below should weigh between 15 and 25 pounds (7 to 12 kilograms).

Gear

☐ **46-55 liter backpack** with a rain shield

☐ **Maps and compass**: the maps in this guide are overview maps, and I strongly recommend getting 1:50,000 hiking maps just in case you're caught out in low visibility conditions or your phone battery dies.

☐ **Hiking poles**: they were super useful for long, flatter sections, snowfields, and river fording for me. I also used them to poke the ground to make sure it was real ground and not just mud.

☐ **Duct tape:** for any small repairs underway.

☐ **Dry bags for packing:** I made the very expensive mistake of not wrapping my laptop in these. Don't make the same.

☐ **First aid kit**, particularly band-aids in case of blisters

Clothing

☐ **Hiking boots**: whether you use high or low hiking boots is up to you.

☐ **Trail runners:** these are optional, but I use mine to give my feet a break from heavy hiking boots, especially on flatter days.

☐ **Rain pants and optional gaiters:** in myr or grasses, the water from plants nearby will soak into your pants if you don't have rain pants or gaiters.

☐ **Rain jacket**

☐ **Windbreaker:** it's frequently misting in the mornings, so if you don't like hiking in your rain jacket, bring a lighter weight jacket to hike in.

☐ **Wool socks, two pairs:** I use one pair of socks for hiking and one pair for the cabin.

☐ **Hiking shorts (optional):** it may be warm enough to hike in shorts.

☐ **Hiking pants** or long underwear to layer under rain pants

☐ **Two sports bras and two pairs of underwear**

☐ **Wool sweater and extra warm jacket**: I wear this when I'm hiking in cooler conditions, and it's always helpful to have in case you

☐ **Hat and gloves**

☐ **Two hiking shirts**: I strongly recommend wool here - it won't get as smelly and will keep you warm even when it gets wet

Cabin Supplies

☐ **Mini towel:** for cabins with showers. The showers are usually single gender but communal, so the towel is handy even if you want to create a little shield to get changed under.

☐ **DNT key:** even if you're not planning to stay in the cabins, it's good to have in case of emergencies

☐ **Sengetøy (sheet set)** or sleep liner: the blankets on the beds are not washed in between guests. You need to bring your own sheets to keep things clean

☐ **Toilet shoes:** about half of the cabins have outdoor toilets, and this keeps you from having to put potentially wet hiking boots back on

☐ **Sleep mask:** there are good curtains in the cabins, but it never gets dark

Food and Drink

☐ **Thermos** for hot drinks

☐ **Water bottle:** there are plenty of rivers and streams to fill up a water bottle as you're hiking

☐ **Candy and snacks**

☐ **Plastic bag for sandwiches**

Tech

☐ **Phone:** I recommend downloading UT, YR, and Hyttebetaling before your hike

☐ **Battery pack**

☐ **Chargers:** many of the self-service cabins only have USB classic charging outlets. If you have a phone with a USB-C charging port, you will want to bring a USB to USB-C charger.

Other

☐ **ID and credit cards:** there's no need to bring cash

☐ **Sunglasses and sunscreen:** if it's sunny, you'll need sunscreen, particularly on the snowfields on Glittertinden and Galdhøpiggen

☐ **Toiletries:** wilderness wash, face wash, toothpaste, toothbrush, contacts, contact lens solution, glasses, hairbrush, hair ties, nail clippers, any medications

☐ **Tiny shovel and toilet paper**

☐ **Extra plastic bags**

Packing List - Winter

What You're Wearing

There's a substantial amount of clothing and gear to wear on the ski trips - much more than on the summer trips:

☐ **Wool base layer, underwear, and socks**: I brought two pairs of socks for really cold days.

☐ **Wool sweater**: on still days, you can just wear this over your base layer to ski in.

☐ **Tights under your pants:** the best strategy is to use long underwear under ski pants. Make sure whatever layer this is is warm.

☐ **Hat, gloves, and neck buff:** I ended up wearing my hat even when I had the hood on my rain jacket up just for the extra warmth on my ears. I made sure my hat fit under my jacket hood.

☐ **Gaiters (optional)**: I passed a lot of people using gaiters, which made sure that snow couldn't get in the top of their ski boots.

☐ **Fjellskis, shoes, and poles**: fjellskis don't have a great translation in English, but they're wide skis with steel edges that can be used for ungroomed terrain. The boots are generally very large and robust - they look more like intense hiking boots than ski boots. If you are doing Jotunheimen's downhills on skis, you will also need a helmet.

☐ **55-70 liter hiking backpack** with a rain shield: if you're planning to camp, you might need something slightly bigger for food storage.

In your bag:

Additional clothing:

☐ **Extra set of clothes**: I took a full set of extra clothes (shirt, underwear, bra, leggings) with me. I wore it in the cabins and when I was letting my main set of clothes dry out.

☐ **Mittens:** gloves were good enough most days, but there were 2-3 days where I needed the super-warm mittens. If the weather forecast is substantially below zero, I'd also take hand warmers.

☐ **Cabin shoes:** inside the cabin, I just wore socks, but the trail runners kept my feet dry-ish on the walk to and from the outdoor bathrooms.

☐ **Down jacket or very thick sweater**: there were several days I ended up layering my top, sweater, down jacket, and then shell on top of it. I like the down jacket because it's light and easy to pack.

Gear:

☐ **Emergency bivvy (vindsekk):** It's essentially a giant waterproof and windproof bag that you can climb into, whether to eat lunch outside of the wind and snow, or if you need to spend the night outside

☐ **Sleeping bag:** in case you get stuck outside overnight. You'll also need your sleeping bag liner or sheet set for sleeping at the cabin.

☐ **Shovel:** for digging down into the snow when you stop for lunch or in case of avalanche. You may also need this if you get to a cabin and the door is blocked by snow - there is a shovel at the cabins, but it is sometimes under the snow.

☐ **Avalanche beacon** if you're going in steep terrain: make sure you know how to use it

☐ **First aid supplies:** I took a ton of bandaids on this trip and was happy that I did. I used an entire box. Otherwise, just the standard stuff here.

☐ **Toiletries:** don't take too much, and keep in mind there's very limited hot water.

☐ **Sitting pad:** for when you stop for lunch and need something to sit on.

☐ **Sunglasses and alpine ski goggles:** it's bright on the snow

☐ **Map and compass:** most of the trails are marked, but there are times where the sticks that mark the routes fall down or turn into reindeer snacks.

☐ **Thermos and plastic bag** for lunch: plastic bags to store sandwiches in, and the thermos to keep water from freezing. I filled my thermos with hot water every morning, and it was fantastic to drink it on the trail.

☐ **Ski wax or skins:** what you'll need depends on your exact skis .

☐ **Headlamp:** the days are short, so the headlamp is doubly important. It's also useful for going to the bathroom at night in the dark.

☐ **Duct tape and Swiss army knife:** in case you have any issues with your gear.

☐ **Snacks:** take some small snacks that you can put in your pockets or the side of your bag, since it's hard to stop and eat in the winters.

☐ **DNT key and membership card:** even if you're not planning to stay in a DNT cabin, take the key in case you need need to duck into a cabin for shelter

☐ **Battery pack** for phone and charger that works with USB outlet: the majority of the cabins have solar power and a USB plug for charging devices. Phone batteries can drain quickly in the cold, especially if you have an iPhone, so make sure to have a backup charger. The solar panels in the self-service cabins can also be intermittent during the darkest season (January and February).

There isn't always service, so download the maps you need before you go.

Some Handy Norwegian Words

Almost all Norwegians speak perfect English. That said, there are times where it's handy to be able to read signs, the weather, or the map.

Hiking and the map

Bratt/meget bratt: steep/very steep

Breen: the glacier

Dalen: the valley

Grusvei: a gravel path

Luftig: steep drop offs on the side of the trail

Kvistet: marked (used for ski trails)

Merket: marked (used for summer trails)

Mobildekning: phone service

Myr: a swampy, wet land covering

Nord, sor, ost, vest: north, south, east, west

Skog: forest

Stein: rocky

Steinur: rocky patches to hike over

Tind/tinden: peak

Vadested: a place that requires wading

Vannet: the water

Varder: cairns

Vatnet: the lake

Vegen: the road

Weather

Bris: breeze

Flom: flood

Lettskyet: barely cloudy

Lyn: lighting

Nedbør: precipitation

Nysnø: new snow (no icy cover yet)

Regn: rain

Weather continued

Skyet: cloudy

Snø: snow

Sol: sun

Soloppgang, solnedgang: sunrise, sunset

Strynregen: very heavy rain

Tåkete: foggy

Torden: thunder

Things in provision rooms

Bønnemix: mixed beans

Erter: peas

Fullkorn: whole grain

Gryte: stew

Hermetikk: shelf-stable boxes

Kaffe: coffee

Kanel: cinnamon

Kokemalt: coffee that needs to be cooked in a kettle

Kjeks: biscuits

Kjøtt: meat

Knekkebrød: crispbread

Kokk uten lokk: cook without a lid

Kylling: chicken

Lapskaus: a Norwegian stew of potatoes and meat

Legg til: add to (e.g. "legg til vann" = "add water")

Linser: lentils

Melkepulver: milk powder (reconstitute with water)

Ost: cheese

Pannekake: pancakes

Food continued

Potetmos: mashed potatoes

Rein: reindeer

Ror godt: stir well

Smør: butter

Sodd: a high calorie stew of pork, potatoes, and some vegetables

Sukker: sugar

Svine: pork

Syltetøy: jam

Turmat: dehydrated hiking food

Vann: water

Cabins

Betjent: serviced (a lodge)

Selvbetjent: self-service (a cabin without staff but with a provision room)

Ubetjent: unserviced (a cabin with beds, propane, and wood, but no food)

Drikkevann: drinking water

Forhåndsbestilt: booked in advance

Hyttefelt: a collection of cabins

Protokoll: the book you have to sign when you arrive at a cabin

Using the Cabins

One of the most amazing things about hiking in Norway is the national cabin network. The Norwegian Trekking Association (DNT) maintains a network of more than 600 cabins spread across the country. It makes it easy to travel deep into the wilderness without carrying food or a tent.

Cabins come in three grades:

Betjent (serviced):

These aren't cabins but full lodges. You'll have a three course meal for dinner, a buffet breakfast with a place to fill your thermos, showers and drying rooms for clothes, and often indoor toilets.

Dinners are served family style, where the staff will bring out giant tureens of soup for a first course, then usually some kind of meat and potatoes, then individual desserts. There's more than enough food for everyone - but make sure to book ahead and alert the cabin if you have dietary restrictions.

The family style dinners mean that you have to go to an assigned dinner time, usually seven o'clock. There's usually assigned seating. People are generally super friendly at dinner and chat about where you've hiked from that day.

Serviced cabins have electricity, but the number of outlets varies. At many cabins, there are only outlets in the common areas. At others, the electricity is turned off after dinner service ends, so don't rely on an overnight charge for your devices.

Serviced cabins also have drying rooms and showers. Drying rooms usually have strong heaters and dehumidifiers that dry out gear overnight. Showers are usually communal for each gender, so if you're shy, try to go at an off-time.

You'll pack lunch for the next day at breakfast. There is parchment paper and sometimes plastic bags for taking sandwiches in - the Norwegians are generally happy to show you how to wrap a sandwich in parchment paper if you need help. The stay at an serviced cabin also includes a thermos fill up for the next morning - they'll let you know at check in if you should leave your thermos at the reception desk or bring it to breakfast to fill it up yourself.

Selvbetjent (self-service)

Self-service cabins are unique to Norway. They're generally smaller than staffed cabins, but come fully stocked with a provisions room, wood for the fireplace, gas for cooking, and cooking supplies. Some have electricity, but it's usually from a single solar panel and is only enough to charge one or two phones. You usually have to fetch and boil water from a nearby water source.

The self-service cabins run on the honor system. They can be unlocked with the DNT key, which you can purchase at a DNT store in Norway, online at their web store ahead of the hike, or at a staffed cabin. To pay for your stay, use the Hyttebetaling app. The app allows you to keep a list of all the supplies you've used and then pay with credit card when you get back into phone service. The app is available in English.

Ubetjent (unserviced)

These are just like self-service cabins, except that there isn't food available in the provision room. There are no ubetjent cabins in this guide. There are two ubetjent cabins in Jotunheimen, but the trails to them are not well maintained and marked, so I have not included them here.

Cabin Etiquette:

When you arrive at an unserviced or self-service cabin, the first thing to do is to unlock the cabin and then take off your shoes. No outdoor shoes are allowed in the cabin to help keep it clean. After that, fill in your information in the besøksprotokoll, a horizontal blue book that asks where you came from, where you're going, and your membership information. After that, you have the right to use the cabin. I generally first start a fire if the cabin is cold, then fetch water to heat up for dinner.

When you leave the cabin in the morning, you'll need to clean up. That means washing all of the dishes, cleaning out the ashes in the fireplace, bringing in fresh wood for the fire, washing the floors in the bedroom and common areas, and any other tidying.

You can use the cabins if you're camping. You'll need to register in the besøksprotokoll and pay for a day visit ("dagsbesøk"). After that, you can cook food or just relax for a bit. Make sure to sweep up and wash the floors after yourself.

Cabin FAQs:

It's not necessary to book in advance for the cabins - if you arrive at the cabin, you'll have a place to sleep, though it might be on a mattress on the floor if it's really busy. I generally don't book cabins in advance so that I have the most flexibility possible to change hiking plans based on the weather.

Book ahead at the serviced cabins if you have dietary restrictions. Because meals are served family style, the cabins need advance notice to be able to accommodate dietary restrictions.

You need to bring a sheet set or sleeping bag liner for use on the beds. The sheets on the bed are not washed in between guests. Sleeping bags are not allowed for hygenic reasons - basically, people climb into them when they're sweaty and don't wash them when they get home.

Most of the serviced cabins are only open during peak spring ski season and the summer hiking season. Jotunheimen has some of the longest opening periods - Gjendesheim is open until October, for example. Self-serviced and unserviced cabins are generally open year round, with exceptions for cabins that are in avalanche-prone terrain. UT.no will have information on cabin opening times.

Joining DNT:

You should absolutely join DNT - the savings on staying in the cabin will cover the cost of the membership in two to three nights. If you are planning to camp, you will still want to join DNT to get a DNT key. You'll need the key if you want to do a day visit or if you end up staying in a cabin during a day with particularly bad weather.

Joining online is a little confusing, and there are updated instructions on the blog. You can also stop by any DNT office in Norway.

Cooking at the cabin:

There is a propane stove and plenty of cooking supplies in the cabins. The food that you'll generally find breaks down into four categories:

Breakfast: knekkebrød (crispbread), oatmeal mix, shelf-stable cheese, pancake mix, leverposti (liver spread), jam and chocolate spread, mackerel in tomatoes, butter, jam, and honey

Dinner: fish soup, peas and carrots, mashed potato mix, lapskaus, rice, bacalo, boxed mixes for Pasta di Parma and Chili Con Carne, pasta, reindeer meatballs, dry red lentils, and crushed tomatoes

Snacks and dessert: chocolate pudding, vanilla sauce, canned fruit in syrup, and biscuits

Misc things: dried hiking food, coffee, tea, hot chocolate, currant drink mix, hiking snacks like knekkebrød sandwiches, sugar, cinnamon

My challenge with cooking at self-service cabins is finding something to bring for lunch the next day. I really load up on breakfast, often mixing vanilla sauce or jam into my oatmeal for the extra calories. I take two or three packages of freeze dried food with me to eat on the trail, in case there isn't shelf-stable cheese and knekkebrød for lunch.

Each cabin has a different selection of food, and if you're late in the season, certain items might be eaten up. If you're vegetarian or gluten-free, make sure to have your own backup food

Cabin Overview

Cabin	Cabin Type	Beds	Pre-bookable beds	Power	Phone Service	
DNT Operated						
Yksendalsbu	Self-service	18	10	Y - 12 volt (USB)	N	
Fannaråken	Serviced	34	34	No	N	
Skogadalsbøen	Serviced	87	87	Y - 220 volt	N	
Fondsbu	Serviced	100	100	Y - 220 volt	Y	
Torfinnsbu	Self-service	28	18	Y - 12 volt (USB)	Y	
Gjendesheim	Serviced	185	185	Y - 220 volt	Y	
Glitterheim	Serviced	137	137	Y - 220 volt	N	
Gjendebu	Serviced	119	119	Y - 220 volt	N	
Leirvassbu	Serviced	205	205	Y - 220 volt	Y	
Olavsbu	Self-service	52	25	Y - 12 volt (USB)	N	
Vettismorki	Self-service	9	5	Y - 12 volt (USB)	N	
Tomashellern	Self-service	14	6	Y - 12 volt (USB)	N	
Private						
Sikkilsdalsseter	Serviced, private	78	78	Y - 220 volt	Y	
Memurubu	Serviced, private	160	160	Y - 220 volt	Y	
Spiterstulen	Serviced, private	280	280	Y - 220 volt	Y	
Sognefjellshytta	Serviced, private	80	80	Y - 220 volt	Y	
Krossbu	Serviced, private	100	100	Y - 220 volt	Y	
Bygdin Høifjeldshotel	Serviced, private	96	96	Y - 220 volt	Y	
Juvasshytta	Serviced, private	75	75	Y - 220 volt	Y	
Hindsæter	Serviced, private	34	34	Y - 220 volt	Y	
Raudbergstulen	Serviced, private	160	160	Y - 220 volt	Y	
Bessheim	Serviced, private	180	180	Y - 220 volt	Y	
Tyinholmen	Serviced, private	80	80	Y - 220 volt	Y	
Vetti Gard Turiststasjon	Serviced, private	38	38	Y - 220 volt	Y	

Drying Room	Shower	Drop point?	Other Notes
N	N	No	I had intermittent phone service, but not reliable
Y	N	No	Must book in advance given limited number of beds
Y	Y	No	Phone service near the stone building about 100 meters from the cabin
Y	Y	Yes	Hosts a music festival in mid-July, which may be booked out. Bus service or boat to Bygdin
N	N	Yes	Scheduled boat service to Bygdin and Fondsbu
Y	Y	Yes	Buses to Lom and Oslo
Y	Y	No	Nearest bus stop is Randsverk, 7 km from the cabin on a road
Y	Y	Yes	Scheduled boat service to Gjendesheim in high season
Y	Y	Yes	Very large, modern cabin - even has wifi. Bus service to Lom.
N	N	No	
N	N	No	I had intermittent phone service
N	N	No	
Y	Y	No	Connects Jotunheimen to Langsua national park
Y	Y	Yes	Scheduled boat service to Gjendesheim in high season
Y	Y	Yes	Has bus service to Lom
Y	Y	Yes	Has bus service to Lom
Y	Y	Yes	Alternative to Sognefjellshytta, has bus service to Lom
Y	Y	Yes	Bus to Beitostølen or boat to Fondsbu
Y	Y	No	Starting point for guided glacier tours up to Galdhøpiggen
Y	Y	Yes	Not in core route network; best for day hikes. Limited bus service
Y	Y	No	Trails go from here to Juvasshytta into Jotunheimen
Y	Y	Yes	Not in core route network; best for day hikes. Limited bus service
Y	Y	Yes	Located near Fondsbu.
Y	Y	No	Used to drop out of the park to Øvre Årdal

FAQs

Can I drink the water underway? Do I need to bring a water filter?
You can drink water directly from streams in Norway, and you'll see the Norwegians doing just that. The cabins also have places where you can fill up water bottles, so no need to bring a water filter. Use common sense - don't drink the water where there are clearly sheep grazing.

Where can I leave luggage?
If you have luggage or items that you don't want to bring on the hike, the best place to leave them is in the city that you'll be returning to after the hike. I usually leave my things in the Oslo airport or train station. There are also luggage storage services in the major cities that will take your things and hold them while you're hiking. There is not storage space at the cabins.

What about luggage transport?
During the summer, you can use the boats for luggage transport - see the logistics section for more details. Book this in advance, and ask at the cabin if you have any questions.

Am I okay just speaking English?
Absolutely. In my entire time in Norway, I have met only three people who couldn't speak English. Jotunheimen especially has lots of foreign guests. The only challenge is that the labels on food in the self-service cabins are only in Norwegian. I've included some key words in the book for reading food labels.

Will I have phone service?
I've listed which cabins have phone service in the cabin amenity section, but generally, you should expect to have phone service in most of the park. Leirvassbu, Spiterstulen, and Gjendesheim even have wifi. Phone service generally varies during the course of the day - even if two cabins both have phone service, the hike in between them may not.

How hard is navigation?
It's not bad at all - the trails are generally really well marked with the characteristic red T and very visible cairns. I used my phone rather than a map and compass. The UT app was a huge help. That being said, I took maps and compass in case my phone died – that turned out to be a good move, because I once broke my phone after falling through a snow bridge in between Leirvassbu to Olavsbu.

When can I go?
July through September are the best times to go. Check SeNorge.no to see the latest snow report. June may still have a lot of snowfields left on the trail, and it will begin snowing in late September on many of the trails.

Is it expensive?
It's about $100/night to stay in a serviced cabin, which includes all food, and $30/night to stay in a self-service cabin. It's a lot cheaper than other hiking trips I've taken because you don't have to pay for a hotel room - you pay by person rather than room. If you want to save on the cost, you can camp some nights rather than staying in the cabins.

Can I do laundry along the way?
You can hand wash clothes at the cabins and then dry them in the drying room or over the fire, but that's it. There are no laundry facilities.

Can I rely on the self-service cabins to have food and supplies?
Yes - I've visited 121 DNT cabins so far and have yet to find one that wasn't stocked. If you have dietary restrictions, though, make sure to bring some backup food. There may not be many options if you are vegetarian or gluten-free.

Can I go in October?
Yes, but stick to lower elevations and be prepared for snow. Pack gear to spend the night outside if necessary. Many of the serviced cabins will be closed.

Should I join DNT?
Yes, absolutely! The membership pays for itself after a couple nights at a cabin, and it's a great way to support the incredible work that DNT does maintaining the trails and cabin system.

Are there visitor centers or rangers?
Not in the same way that you find in American national parks. If you want to ask questions, reach out to a DNT Tursenteret or ask the staff at the cabin.

Do I need a permit to hike or camp?
Nope! In fact, you can just show up at the cabin and ask for a place to sleep. That's one of the great things about Norway - you have a lot of flexibility in choosing your route based on the weather and trail conditions.

I can't find maps online. Where can I buy them?
You can purchase them at the serviced cabins, online at the DNT online shop (dntbutikken.no), or at any DNT office or most sporting goods stores in Norway. Same for the DNT key - I recommend buying it in Norway, because shipping is quite expensive from the online store if you're only buying the DNT key.

Can I bring my dog?
It's possible to bring your dog hiking with you. You will need to make reservations in the cabins ahead of time - dogs are not allowed in most areas of the cabin, and you will need to book a specific dog-friendly room. Bring the supplies necessary for your dog to spend the night outside - unlike for humans, there's no guarantee of space for a dog.

Also note that there is a leash law in effect in the park from April 1st to October 1st. That applies to all dogs, even small dogs.

Can I use a drone to film?
No. Drone use is not permitted in national parks or in protected nature areas.

Can I choose my menu at the serviced cabins?
Nope. Dinner is served family style. If you have dietary restrictions, notify the cabin staff in advance so that they can accommodate.

Are there bears?
Nope! One of the great things about hiking in Norway is that you don't need to bring pepper spray or bear repellent for your hike. In fact, it's illegal to bring bear spray into the country, as it's considered a restricted weapon. There are no animals that you need to worry about, other than domestic grazing animals (e.g. cows and sheep).

How accurate are the time estimates in the book?
The time estimates here are taken from ut.no and give the estimated time for an average Norwegian hiker carrying a backpack. If you're not used to hiking, you may be slower.

What's the biggest mistake people make on this hike?
Underestimating how cold and wet it can be. Make sure you have enough layers to keep warm!

Fjellvettreglene (Norwegian Mountain Code)

The Norwegian Mountain Code contains the guidelines for having a safe trip in the Norwegian mountains. They're considered an important part of Norwegian cultural heritage and were introduced after a spate of fatal accidents in 1950.

1. Plan your trip and inform others about the route you have selected.

2. Adapt the planned routes according to ability and conditions.

3. Pay attention to the weather and the avalanche warnings.

4. Be prepared for bad weather and frost, even on short trips.

5. Bring the necessary equipment so you can help yourself and others.

6. Choose safe routes. Recognize avalanche terrain and unsafe ice.

7. Use a map and a compass. Always know where you are.

8. Don't be ashamed to turn around.

9. Conserve your energy and seek shelter if necessary.

Sarah Rowe has solo hiked more than 4,500 kilometers across 24 countries, with a focus on Norway and Austria. She's the recipient of DNT's golden key, having visited more than 100 DNT cabins, and has hiked seven of DNT's thirteen SignaTUR tours.

When she's not out hiking, she's writing about it on her blog, Solo Female Wanderer, drinking coffee, and planning the next adventure. She lives in London.

Questions or comments? You can reach her at sarah@solofemalewanderer.com

www.ingramcontent.com/pod-product-compliance
Lightning Source LLC
Chambersburg PA
CBHW051224120626
46547CB00013B/1496